Art of
Successful Parenting

Published by :
Lotus Press Publishers & Distributors

Art of Successful Parenting

Priyanka Narang

Lotus PRESS

4735/22, Prakash Deep Building
Ansari Road, Darya Ganj,
New Delhi - 110002

Lotus Press Publishers & Distributors
Unit No. 220, 2nd Floor, 4735/22, Prakash Deep Building,
Ansari Road, Darya Ganj, New Delhi-110002
Ph.: 23280047, 41325510, 98118-38000
• E-mail : lotuspress1984@gmail.com
www.lotuspress.co.in

Art of Successful Parenting

ISBN: 978-81-8382-230-5

Printed & Published by : **Lotus Press Publisher & Distributors,** New Delhi-02

Preface

Every human being is born with a special purpose that is to be fulfilled. His/her life here on the planet is to discover, understand, learn and fulfil her destiny. So it becomes inevitable that parents need to help the child to accomplish this. To deny or curb this instinct in the child in fulfilling her life's mission would mean going against the very principle of evolution, the essence of creation. Lack of knowledge about child development causes misery and conflict in us bringing pain to ourselves and others. Hence there is a need to understand and learn the art of parenting to have peace and harmony.

To be an excellent father or mother requires a great deal of understanding oneself and also the children. This book reveals to you the art of handling children, making them more self-disciplined, self-motivated and self-directed. The parents create a perfect role model. The book describes how to create a quality culture in children and gives you a set of principles to be followed in order to understand the needs, emotions and problems of the kids and live together happily.

Parenting is a great responsibility and it involves handling numerous problems. It is more than the management, leadership. If you are a success in this you can be success in any job, situation, circumstances. This book is an excellent guide on raising kids, from conception to adulthood. Lessons learnt here can be applied anywhere with phenomenal success.

Author

Contents

1

Introduction to Parenting

Parenting is the greatest responsibility that any couple can take on. It involves careful attention to every need of the child in order to ensure that he has a complete and all round development. Young parents face an overwhelming responsibility to monitor their child's health and simultaneously begin the process of moulding the child into a sensitive, curious and bright individual. Daunting, as the entire process of bringing up a child may seem, it is a charge that has successfully been accomplished by parents over the centuries.

Being a parent is one of the most fulfilling experiences a person can have. There is a natural instinct that seems to come to a new parent, but there are bits of advice that can help when you are challenged in the growing up years. The most important thing however, that any parent can give their child, is a sense of being loved.

In India, parenting is based on values. Women living in joint families are provided with the traditional guidance of nurturing the fetus. Traditionally, the pregnant women would be encouraged to attend regular prayer meets, listen to soft and calming music, read tales from Indian mythology, as well as the scriptures. They felt that everything that would engage the mother's mind in calming thoughts would be good food for the fetus's developing mind. This is not only a practice amongst Hindus, but every religion provides such guidance to women who are pregnant.

Effective parenting skills are a combination of love and logic. Sometimes mothers tend to overlook the need to be practical and logical, letting their young ones get away with bad behaviour. And on the other hand some mothers tend to be so practical in their ways that children grow up feeling unloved. Parenting with love and logic is not about upbringing beyond the birth, but even while the baby is developing in the womb. While ancient scriptures contain numerous tales to prove that impressions are created in the human mind while still in the womb; today, numerous researches in modern sciences are proving the same through the various experiments.

Good parenting is virtue that is inbuilt in every mother. However, sometimes due to excessive stress and tension, mothers tend to lose control over their emotions and deal with the children wrongly. And unfortunately children tend to carry forward the negative impressions into their adult life, rather than all the positives the parents have done. Thus, it is important that a mother is always in control of her emotions and mental state of mind. And this awareness will always help her inculcate good values in the child.

As part of the prenatal development, it has been an age-old practice to listen to good soothing music as well as make the pregnant one read value-based books. There is a lot of literature that promotes the proper *garbh sanskar,* which means values for the fetus. One needs to remember that the first set of impressions is what the fetus gathers, and the experience of the womb is the seed of the rest of the human life.

Role of Parents in Child Upbringing

In the grooming of a child, parents play a very vital rọle. But anomalies arise, when the role of the parents are not set out right. It has been the long held view that in the bringing up of a child, the mother reserves the prime responsibility and the father has to take care of the family as a whole, with respect to other aspects, which do not directly pertain to the upbringing of the child. But this is a crass misconception.

Parents influence the lives of their children in every aspect and leave an impression which remains throughout their lives. For one very common instance, it is but natural that a boy aspires to imitate his father in driving or a daughter desires to acquire the culinary expertise from her mother. The seeds of thought which parents sow in the minds of their children will go a long way in defining their courses of lives.

It is not to be overlooked that when a child enters this world as a new tenant, its mind remains a *tabula rasa*. It is the parents who imbue the morals (or otherwise) into their minds. As such, the attitudes of the parents will certainly be reflected in the activities of their children. Therefore, when a child sees the world around it through the eyes of its parents, it is but natural that its world takes up the shape of the perspectives of its parents.

This could be the sole reason, why parents are required to be role models for their children and it is indeed their responsibility to see that they set fine standards for their children to grow up, emulate and groom into dignified individuals.

The ill-effects of sheer negligence on the part of the parents in taking care of the children will be appalling. It is no exaggeration to point out that many children end up being juvenile derelicts, thanks to the insouciance of their parents in setting up moral standards for them.

Hence, it is high time parents realised the significance of their roles in bringing up their children and the price which they have to pay for their inaction.

Parents are the first and the best teachers for any child. The teacher may praise or punish, behave unruly or orderly, but ultimately the test is set for the children. Thus, parents deserve kudos for shaping up a responsible individual and they have to warrant for any unacceptable behaviour of their children as well.

It is the responsibility of the parent to:

- make a commitment for the rest of your life to your child(ren).
- protect them for as long as they need it.
- be there for them through good and bad.
- love them, but don't spoil them. They have to be responsible for their actions.
- teach them wisely about being polite, respect for others and themselves.
- take time out of your busy week to have fun with them.
- teach them things throughout their life while living at home.
- tell them stories about you growing up (the funnier the better.)
- teach them to obey rules around the house to prepare them for the future.
- build their confidence up.
- teach them that as long as they've tried their very best they are never a loser.
- teach them how to treat other beings.

– give them a good solid belief in God.

– teach them about nature and to respect it. Teach them to have compassion and not to label people quickly.

– know that your child(ren) will want to try their independence and be a pain in the butt at times.

– know when to let your children go and become independent.

The responsibilities of the parents are innumerous. Parenthood can be difficult at best and parents don't have an instruction book given to them to raise their children so mistakes will be made. There are always those magic words, "I was wrong, and I'm sorry." As long as parents try their very best to bring their children up then they have done themselves proud and have brought up a strong and confident child(ren.)

Responsibility of Mothers

Parents have a sacred duty to rear their children in love and righteousness, to provide for their physical and spiritual needs, to teach them to love and serve one another, to observe the commandments of God and to be law-abiding citizens wherever they live.

Mother as Nurturer

Biologically, mothers have been given the hallowed opportunity to bear children. Because they nurture the developing child in their own bodies, they almost always feel a compelling drive to protect the new, entirely dependent life they've given birth to. Most mothers also feel inherent motivation to comfort and guide their child. So it's natural in the vast majority of cases that a mother becomes her child's primary caregiver, especially during the first few years of life.

Infants and small children are completely dependent on their caregivers to survive. As a child grows, she becomes less physically dependent but continues to need the nurturing care of her mother, including acceptance, love, understanding, and teaching. These many hours of care each day make mothers most often the person closest to their children and the person with greatest influence. Experiences with mother powerfully shape a child's perspective, attitudes, and sense of self. Without good nurturing in these early stages, a child's development can be seriously harmed.

Mother's Contributions

Mothering is among the most complex and demanding work imaginable. Being a mother can require learning the stages of a child's development, preparing nutritionally balanced meals, and helping with algebra. The role is made even more complex by the need for individualised parenting. As a mother spends quantity and quality time with each child, she learns each child's individual needs and the best way to lovingly fill those needs.

Studies show mothers approach parenting differently than do fathers. While fathers tend to be more physical with their children, wrestling and tickling and playing ball, mothers tend to talk with their children more, explore feelings, and foster social skills. As children share what's going on in their lives in casual conversation, mother gets the chance to gently guide, teach, and advise. When she does this well, her children come to see her as their number one supporter.

Motherhood often is seen as a submissive role with few rewards. In a world that values material possessions so highly, the intangible and unpaid work of mothers can seem unimportant. A paycheck may become attractive because it may help Mom feel more valued and allows kids to have a higher standard of living. Women who buy into these ideas might start to think they're not needed at home. Maybe their children can take care of themselves or someone else can care for them just as well as they can. A mother might decide her children need the material advantages of life more than they need her presence.

But children need their mothers. No material possession can replace a mother who is present and available to her children. They thrive when mother is home when they are, when she's loving and accepting, and when she listens to them and tries to understand. While children might complain if they don't have name-brand clothes or the latest technical gadget, as they mature they come to understand and deeply appreciate the gift of a mother who was present for them.

Studies show that women who are mothers believe their lives have greater meaning than women who don't have children. It's difficult to measure the value of unselfishly giving of yourself to a child who depends on you.

Responsibility of Fathers

Every man who fathers a child has a moral and sacred responsibility to his son or daughter. By divine design, fathers are to preside over their families in love and righteousness and are responsible to provide the necessities of life and protection for their families.

Fathering can be very rewarding—and very demanding. "From a spiritual perspective, fathering is both a joyous blessing and a challenging, sacred responsibility". A father's active involvement profoundly affects his children and generations to come. Children who have fathers who are involved in their lives—whether the children are biological, adopted, or step children—have a better chance of excelling socially, emotionally, and academically.

Children need fathers to provide them with the necessities of life, such as wholesome food, clothing, and shelter in a safe neighbourhood (whether he lives with his children or not). As a father provides this stability, his children feel secure and have higher self-worth. They're better able to develop normally, including performing well in school, developing healthy relationships with peers, and achieving in their individual interests.

A father is also responsible for providing emotional, social, and spiritual protection and support for his family. Children need affection from their fathers, both physical and verbal. They need reassurance, kind and loving discipline, and spiritual leadership.

Active participation in religion often helps fathers be more involved with their children. Religious fathers are more likely to be positively involved physically, mentally, and emotionally with their children. Religion can help men see that being a father is a "sacred service to God and not just a social role".

Not only children benefit when a father is involved. Their father, too, benefits. As his children look to him as an example of how to express feelings and emotions, he learns about empathy, sensitivity to emotions, and how to express his own emotions. When a father hears his child crying or knows his child is hungry, he becomes more caring and nurturing and learns to put others' needs ahead of his own.

Many men feel there are barriers that keep them from being involved. They might feel inadequate as a provider or unprepared for the emotional demands of fatherhood. Some have false beliefs about the role of fathers, such as the idea that mothers should provide all the nurturing and fathers should simply provide materially. All these barriers can be overcome by learning more about fatherhood through books, community support groups, and other men who are good fathers.

Goals of Parenting

Parenting is the process of promoting and supporting the physical, emotional, social, and intellectual development of a child from infancy to adulthood. Parenting refers to the activity of raising a child rather than the biological relationship.

The goals of human parenting are debated. Usually, parental figures provide for a child's physical needs, protect them from harm, and impart in them skills and cultural values until they reach legal adulthood, usually after adolescence. Among non-human species, parenting is usually less lengthy and complicated, though mammals tend to nurture their young extensively. The degree of attention parents invest in their offspring is largely inversely proportional to the number of offspring the average adult in the species produces.

There is general consensus around parents providing the basic necessities, with increasing interest in children's rights within the home environment.

Table 1. Child needs and Parental tasks

Need	Parental task
Physical security—The safety of a child's body and life.	• Provide physical safety: shelter, clothes, nourishment • To protect a child from dangers; physical care • To care for a child's health
Physical development—Appropriate conditions for a healthy growth of a child	• To provide a child with the means to develop physically • To train the body of a child, to introduce to exercise • To develop habits of health
Intellectual security—The conditions in which a child's mind can develop	• Provide an atmosphere of peace and justice and respect to one's dignity • Provide an environment without fear, threat, and abuse

Intellectual development—Providing opportunity to a child to learn	• Reading, writing, calculating etc. • Support and/or provide school related learning • Teach social skills and etiquette • Moral and spiritual development. As well as creating an ethics and value systems with social norms that contribute to the child's beliefs, culture; and customs
Emotional security—To help protect a child's psyche	• Provide a safe loving environment • Give a child a sense of being loved, being needed, welcomed • Emotional support, encouragement • Attachment, caressing, hugging, touch, etc.
Emotional development—Developing the child's ability to love, care, help, etc.	• Show empathy and compassion to younger, weaker and sicker, etc • Caring for others, helping grandparents, etc.

Good children are a product of the real goal of parenting: *mature character*. When children grow up with mature character, they are able to take their place as adults in the world and function properly in all areas of life. Character growth is the main goal of child rearing.

But what is character? For some, the word character brings to mind pictures of a person who has integrity, takes responsibility for her life, and stands up for the right thing. Others may see character as the child's personality—those attributes that make her unique, such as energy level, interests, and a sense of humour.

People with mature character do have traits of integrity, responsibility and courage, but we understand character in a bigger-picture way. We view character as the structures and abilities within ourselves that make up how we operate in life. In other words, character is the sum of our abilities to deal with life as God designed us to. Reality makes certain demands on us, for example, to relate to other people in good ways, to do what we say we will do, to take ownership of our own mistakes, and to solve our own problems. Our success (or failure) in meeting these demands shows our level of character development.

You may know adults who look good and perform well but have character flaws. These character flaws—a bad temper, a tendency to withdraw, or self-centredness—rear their ugly heads over and over again to diminish that person's life experience. More often than not, these flaws began in childhood and continued on in adulthood. This is why parenting is so critical; childhood is the time when character strengths and weaknesses are laid down.

Process of Parenting

Parenthood is a feeling of completeness. It is a thread woven of memories. Memories of happy and sad times, of pain and of joy. Parenthood is a continuous activity, it is a process in itself. Parenthood process is irreversible. We all take birth, grow up, grow old and finally find peace in God. This is a human life-cycle, which cannot be altered, so is parenting process. Once a parent, is a parent forever. Parenting process helps evolve a person, as a child, as a parent and above all as a human being. Parenting process affects our personality, our attitude towards life over time and throughout the course of the life-cycle.

The process of evolving in parenthood, becoming a parent is a gratifying and pleasing experience but also very demanding and nerve-racking. We would request and suggest that parenting process is the right time to greet and embrace the change of a lifetime. Someone, very rightly said, it is tough to understand the parenting process unless you become a parent yourselves.

The parent must understand the significance of a mother and a father in the life of your child. It is usually assumed that a mother plays most important role in parenting process. But, to completely neglect a fathers position in parenting process is not right. An affectionate, time devoting father, who participates in the child's daily activities, help shape up the child's personality in a manner which mother cannot do. This paternal element of closeness in parenting process helps develop the child emotionally as well as mentally. Parenting process, thus emphasises that love of both the parents is a healthy and healing experience for the child. We would suggest that if the child is considered to be fruit of parenting process, mother and father are the roots of parenting process.

A very important understanding and learning of parenting process is that, as a parent you are always at the giving side of the relation. Parenting process states that you should not expect returns from your children. To give all your love and support to your child, is an eternal element of parenting process.

The other important key factor of parenting process is that the parent must learn a fact that children learn what they see. As a parent you must preach only what you proclaim, you yourselves know. Children are a mirror of what they see. So being a parent, as a learning of parenting process, parent must not introduce children to tension, confusion in life or any sort of harsh or fight behaviour, at least through the family. Children replicate what they see, so mark your actions and words; this is the base of parenting process.

At the crux of parenting process, be positive in your attitude, and your child will follow. Be hopeful, full of energy and life, accept challenges, strive to achieve the perfection, this way the parenting process will help shape-up the personality and identity of your child.

Prenatal Parenting

During pregnancy the unborn child is affected by many decisions his or her parents make, particularly choices linked to their lifestyle. The health and diet decisions of the mother can have either a positive or negative impact on the child during prenatal parenting.

Many people believe that parenting begins with birth, but the mother begins raising and nurturing a child well before birth. Scientific evidence indicates that from the fifth month on, the unborn baby is able to hear sound, be aware of motion, and possibly exhibit short-term memory. Several studies show evidence that the unborn baby can become familiar with his or her parents' voices. Other research indicates that by the seventh month, external schedule cues influence the unborn baby's sleep habits. Based on this evidence, parenting actually begins well before birth. Depending on how many children the mother carries also determines the amount of care needed during prenatal and post-natal periods.

Parenting of Newborns and Infants

Newborn parenting, up to one month of age, is where the responsibilities of parenthood begins. A newborn's basic needs are food, sleep, comfort and cleaning which the parent provides. An infant's only form of communication is crying, and attentive parents will begin to recognise different types of crying which represent different needs such as hunger, discomfort, boredom, or loneliness. Newborns and young infants require feedings every few hours which is disruptive to adult sleep cycles. They respond enthusiastically to soft stroking, cuddling and caressing. Gentle rocking back and forth often calms a crying infant, as do massages and warm baths. Newborns may comfort themselves by sucking their thumb or a pacifier. The need to suckle is instinctive and allows newborns to feed. Breastfeeding is the recommended method of feeding by all major infant health organisations. If breastfeeding is not possible or desired, bottle feeding is a common alternative. Other alternatives include feeding breastmilk or formula with a cup, spoon, feeding syringe, or nursing supplementer.

The forming of attachments is considered to be the foundation of the infant/child's capacity to form and conduct relationships throughout life. Attachment is not the same as love and/or affection although they often go together. Attachment and attachment behaviours tend to develop between the age of 6 months and 3 years. A lack of attachment or a seriously disrupted capacity for attachment could potentially amount to serious disorders.

Until infants learn to walk, between 10 and 14 months, they are carried in the arms, held in slings or baby carriers, or transported in baby carriages or strollers. Upon learning to walk the child is then known as a toddler.

Toddler Parenting

Toddlers are much more active than infants and are challenged with learning how to do simple tasks by themselves. At this stage, parents are heavily involved in showing the child how to do things rather than just doing things for them, and the child will often mimic the parents. Toddlers need help to build their vocabulary, increase their communications skills, and manage their emotions. Toddlers will also begin to understand social etiquette such as being polite and taking turns.

Toddlers are very curious about the world around them and eager to explore it. They seek greater independence and responsibility and may become frustrated when things do not go they way they want or expect. Tantrums begin at this stage, which is sometimes referred to as the 'Terrible Twos'. Tantrums are often caused by the child's frustration over the particular situation, sometimes simply not being able to communicate properly. Parents of toddlers are expected to help guide and teach the child, establish basic routines (such as washing hands before meals, brushing teeth before bed), and increase the child's responsibilities.

Child Parenting

Younger children are becoming more independent and are beginning to build friendships. They are able to reason and can make their own decisions given hypothetical situations. Young children demand constant attention, but will learn how to deal with boredom and be able to play independently. They also enjoy helping and feeling useful and able. Parents may assist their child by encouraging social interactions and modelling proper social behaviours. A large part of learning in the early years comes from being involved in activities and household duties. Parents who observe their children in play or join with them in child-driven play have the opportunity to glimpse into their children's world, learn to communicate more effectively with their children and are given another setting to offer gentle, nurturing guidance. Parents are also teaching their children health, hygiene, and eating habits through instruction and by example.

Parents are expected to make decisions about their child's education. Parenting styles in this area diverge greatly at this stage with some parents becoming heavily involved in arranging organised activities and early learning programmes. Other parents choose to let the child develop with few organised activities.

Children begin to learn responsibility, and consequences of their actions, with parental assistance. Some parents provide a small allowance that increases with age to help teach children the value of money and how to be responsible with it. Parents who are consistent and fair with their discipline, who openly communicate and offer explanations to their children, and who do not neglect the needs of their children in some way often find they have fewer problems with their children as they mature.

Parenting Adolescents

During adolescence children are beginning to form their identity and are testing and developing the interpersonal and occupational roles that they will assume as adults. Although adolescents look to peers and adults outside of the family for guidance and models for how to behave, parents remain influential in their development. Parents often feel isolated and alone in parenting adolescents, but they should still make efforts to be aware of their adolescents activities, provide guidance, direction, and consultation. Adolescence can be a time of high risk for children, where newfound freedoms can result in decisions that drastically openup or closeoff life opportunities. Parental issues at this stage of parenting include dealing with "rebellious" teenagers, who didn't know freedom while they were smaller.

Parenting Young Adults

Young adults—as children become young adults their personalities show the result of successful or unsuccessful parenting. Especially it is noticeable when young adults make their independent life decisions about their education, work and choosing mates for friendship or marriage. Parenting doesn't stop when children grow up and age. Parents always remain to be parents for old children. Their relationship continues developing if both parties want to keep it or improve. The parenting issues may include the relationship with grandchildren and stepchildren.

Parent's Influence on Children

The parent-child relationship is the most important relationship the child has. Different parental styles lead to various ways we interact with our children and is an important component that shapes the child's views about themselves and their world.

Most parents hardly appreciate the degree of responsibility they owe their children. They are often so busy as bread winners striving to earn money for the upkeep of their families. A French proverb states: "a father is a banker provided by nature". The reality staring us in the face is that the children's upbringing is as important as earning incomes for the maintenance of children.

Social counsellors take great pains to educate parents on their duties but the pressure of contemporary survival diverts attention to the critical factor of making ends meet.

One verse of the Bible conjures prime attention: "train up a child in the way he should go and when he is old he will not depart from it." However, no child is ever perfect. What is important is to be proud of the child you breed. Examples are better than precepts. Children are generally sensitive and see parents as role models for emulation.

A lot has to be done to counter the evil effect of peer pressures. Parents should exercise calm, loving persistence as well as understanding with considerable patience. No matter how irritating their conduct may be, parental guidance is indispensable. Nothing should be left to chance. Drug education is as necessary as sex education. Parents must watch the company their children keep and the social parties they attend. The increasing incidence of AIDS epidemic, alcoholism and cocaine consumption among youths call for utmost caution and apprehension.

There is no limit to parental monitoring and tutoring. Motivating children who behave well should come in intrinsic rewards and open commendation. John Smith admonishes: "building strong and honest relationship with your children is a vital ingredient of parenting".

Children learn integrity, sincerity, transparency and accountability from parental comportment and character. The most daunting period with children is when they start to assert their identity. It is regarded as a period where they demand freedom as a matter of course. This conflict should be handled with maturity and tact.

Direct interactions, identification, and knowledge of the accomplishments of family members are three important ways in which families influence children. The first mechanism has its greatest effect on intellectual development and character traits, especially the control of aggression and motivation for achievement. The second and third mechanisms, identification and family myths, have a greater influence on the child's confidence or doubt about his/her talent and, therefore, on the child's expectation of future success or failure.

Parental qualities contribute to a child's psychological profile, rather than to conclude that family conditions determine a particular outcome. An infant's secure attachment to a parent does not guarantee a benevolent outcome or protect a child against psychological problems later in life, but the secure attachment probably constrains the likelihood of producing an adult who is homeless.

2

Styles of Parenting

Developmental psychologists have long been interested in how parents impact child development. However, finding actual cause-and-effect links between specific actions of parents and later behaviour of children is very difficult. Some children raised in dramatically different environments can later grow up to have remarkably similar personalities. Conversely, children who share a home and are raised in the same environment can grow up to have astonishingly different personalities than one another. Despite these challenges, researchers have uncovered convincing links between parenting styles and the effects these styles have on children.

A parenting style is a psychological construct representing standard strategies that parents use in their child rearing. Most parents aim to raise successful, happy children, although some may prefer to enjoy their own lives, while others aim for the maximum number of children without regard to their happiness. There are many views on the best ways to achieve this, as well as differing levels of time and effort that parents are willing to invest. The degree to which a child's education is part of parenting is a further matter of debate.

One of the biggest effects on parenting is socioeconomic status, in reference with ethnicity and culture as well. For example, living in a dangerous neighbourhood could make a parent authoritarian due to fear of their environment. Many parents choose a combination of parenting styles, and these may evolve over time as the children develop their own personalities and move through life's stages. Parenting style is largely affected by the influence of one's own parents and culture. "Most parents learn parenting practices from their own parents—some they accept, some they discard." Both the parents' and children's temperaments affect the style of parenting. Parents who are more highly educated tend to have better jobs, financial security, and this lack of potential stressors has a significant affect on parenting.

There is no single or definitive model of parenting. What may be right for one family or one child may not be suitable for another. With authoritarian and permissive (indulgent) parenting on opposite sides of the spectrum, most conventional and modern models of parenting fall somewhere in between. The model or style that parents employ depends partly on how they themselves were reared, what they consider good parenting, the child's temperament, their current environmental situation, and whether they place more importance on their own needs or whether they are striving to further their child's future success. Parents who place greater importance on the child's physical security may be more authoritarian, while parents who are more concerned with intellectual development may push their children into a number of organised extracurricular activities such as music and language lessons.

Theories of Child Rearing

One of the best known theories of parenting style was developed by Diana Baumrind. She proposed that parents fall into one of three categories: authoritarian (telling their children exactly what to do), indulgent (allowing their children to do whatever they wish), or authoritative (providing rules and guidance without being overbearing). The theory was later extended to include negligent parents (disregarding the children, and focusing on other interests). A number of ethical parenting styles have been proposed, some based on the authoritarian model of strict obedience to scriptural law (for example in the Bible), others based on empathy with the emotional state of a child.

The intensity of parental involvement remains a matter of debate. At opposite extremes are Slow parenting in which parents stand back, merely supporting their children in doing what they want to do as independent individuals (but guiding them when the children are not developing healthy attitudes), versus Concerted cultivation in which children are driven to attend a maximum number of lessons and organised activities, each designed to teach them a valuable skill which the parent has decided for them.

Other theorists, mainly from the twentieth century, have focused on how children develop and have had a significant impact on childhood education and how parents rear their children.

Jean Piaget's theory of cognitive development describes how children represent and reason about the world. This is a developmental stage theory that consists of a sensorimotor stage, preoperational stage, concrete operational stage, and formal operational stage. Piaget was a pioneer in the field of child development and continues to influence parents, educators and other theorists.

Erik Erikson, a developmental psychologist, proposed eight life stages through which each person must develop. In each stage, they must understand and balance two conflicting forces, and so parents might choose a series of parenting styles that helps each child as appropriate at each stage. The first five of his eight stages occur in childhood: The virtue of hope requires balancing trust with mistrust, and typically occurs from birth to one year old. Will balances autonomy with shame and doubt around the ages of two to three. Purpose balances initiative with guilt around the ages of four to six years. Competence balances industry against inferiority around ages 7 to 12. Fidelity contrasts identity with role confusion, in ages 13 to 19. The remaining adult virtues are love, care and wisdom.

Rudolf Dreikurs believed that pre-adolescent children's misbehaviour was caused by their unfulfilled wish to be a member of a social group. He argued that they then act out a sequence of four mistaken goals: first they seek attention. If they do not get it, they aim for power, then revenge and finally feel inadequate. This theory is used in education as well as parenting, forming a valuable theory upon which to manage misbehaviour. Other parenting techniques should also be used to encourage learning and happiness.

Baumrind's Parenting Styles

During the early 1960s, psychologist Diana Baumrind conducted a study on more than 100 preschool-age children. Using naturalistic observation, parental interviews and other research methods, she identified four important dimensions of parenting:

1. Disciplinary strategies.
2. Warmth and nurturance.
3. Communication styles.
4. Expectations of maturity and control.

Based on these dimensions, Baumrind suggested that the majority of parents display one of three different parenting styles. Further research by also suggested the addition of a fourth parenting style.

"Baumrind believes that parents should be neither punitive nor aloof." Rather, they should develop rules for their children and be affectionate with them. In her research she identified three main parenting styles in early child development: authoritative, authoritarian, and permissive. Maccoby and Martin expanded the styles to four: authoritative, authoritarian, indulgent and neglectful. These four styles of parenting involve combinations of acceptance and responsiveness on the one hand and demand and control on the other. These four styles are described below.

These parenting styles are meant to describe normal variations in parenting, not deviant parenting, such as might be observed in abusive homes. Most parents do not fall neatly in one category, but fall in the middle, showing characteristics of more than one style.

Authoritative Parenting

Authoritative parenting, also called balanced parenting, is characterised by a child-centred approach that holds high expectations of maturity, compliance to parental rules and directions, while allowing for an open dialogue about those rules and behaviours between the parent and child. Authoritative parenting encourages children to be independent but still places limits and controls on their actions. Extensive verbal give-and-take is allowed, and parents are warm and nurturant toward the child. Authoritative parents are not usually as controlling, allowing the child to explore more freely, thus having them make their own decisions based upon their own reasoning.

Authoritative parents set limits, demand maturity, but when punishing a child, the parent will always explain his or her motive for their punishment. Their punishments are measured and consistent in discipline, not harsh or arbitrary. Parents will set clear standards for their children, monitor limits that they set, and also allow children to develop autonomy. They also expect mature, independent, and age-appropriate behaviour of children. They are attentive to their children's needs and concerns, and will typically forgive instead of punishing if a child falls short. This is supposed to result in children having a higher self-esteem and independence because of the democratic give-take nature of the Authoritative parenting style.

Children whose parents are authoritative are often cheerful, self-controlled, self-reliant, and achievement–oriented; they maintain friendly relations with peers, cooperate with adults, and cope well with stress. These children also do well in school and have a high academic competence. These children are usually liked by teachers and peers, especially in cultures where individual initiative is valued. This is the most recommended style of parenting by child-rearing experts.

Authoritarian Parenting

Authoritarian parenting, also called strict, is characterised by high expectations of conformity and compliance to parental rules and directions, that does not allow for open dialogue between parent and child. Authoritarian parenting is a restrictive, punitive style in which parents exhort the child to follow their directions and to respect their work and effort. Authoritarian parents expect much of their child but do not explain the reasoning for the rules or boundaries, unlike the Authoritative parent. Authoritarian parents are unresponsive to children's needs, and are most likely to spank a child as a form of punishment instead of grounding a child. They also expect children to comply with their demands no questions asked. The resulting children from this type of parenting are thought to lack social competence as the parent generally predicts what the child should do instead of allowing the child to choose by him or herself. The children also rarely take initiatives. Studies show that children tend to be socially withdrawn and look to others to decide what's right, thus lacking social independence. These children tend to have low self-esteem, low self-confidence and lack of social academic competence.

Children of authoritarian parents are often unhappy, fearful, and anxious about comparing themselves with others; they often tend to fail to initiate activity and have weak communication skills. These children lack spontaneity and lack curiosity. It is noteworthy to mention, that some children might also rebel by openly defying the parents by leaving home at a younger age, partaking in drugs, alcohol, and sexual behaviour at a much younger age than some of their peers as well, dating and/or marrying a partner whom they know their parents would disapprove of, and often might be estranged from their parents during adulthood. Further, boys are often more negatively impacted by authoritarian parenting than are girls.

Many people who grew up with authoritarian parents have sometimes mentioned feeling a sense of relief whenever one (or both) of their parents died. Nonetheless, researchers have found that in some cultures and ethnic groups, aspects of authoritarian style may be associated with more positive child outcomes that Baumrind predicts.

Indulgent Parenting

Indulgent parenting, also called permissive, non-directive

or lenient, is characterised as having few behavioural expectations for the child and is characterised by warm affect. Indulgent parenting is a style of parenting in which parents are very involved with their children but place few demands or controls on them. Parents are nurturing and accepting, and are very responsive to the child's needs and wishes. This type of parent simply wants the child to like him or her at the end of the day and will do anything the child requests to do. Indulgent parents do not require children to regulate themselves or behave appropriately, and some parents find it easier to communicate with their children in this way.

Children of permissive parents are impulsive, have low levels of school achievement, and as adolescents, engage more in misconduct and drug use. Sometimes the resulting children are rarely (if ever) punished and are generally immature. But in the better cases they are independent and are willing to learn and accept defeat. They are able to live life without the help of someone else. The children cannot control their impulses and do not accept the responsibility for their own actions. When in trouble, the child will simply blame someone else even if it was his or her own fault. Indulgent parents raise unhappy children who lack self-control, especially in the give-and-take of peer relationships. Inadequate emotional regulation makes them immature and impedes friendships.

Children never learn to control their own behaviour and always expect to get their way. They tend to live and remain close to where they grew up, still dependent, in early adulthood. However, like a child raised in an authoritative setting and unlike a child raised in an authoritarian setting the children will often continue to have a close and loving relationship with the parents in adulthood. However, children whose parents are indulgent rarely learn respect for others and have difficulty controlling their behaviour. They might be domineering, egocentric, noncompliant, and have difficulties in peer relations.

Neglectful Parenting

Neglectful parenting is also called uninvolved, disengaged, detached, dismissive, nonconformist or hands-off. The parents are low in warmth and control, are generally not involved in their child's life, are disengaged, undemanding, low in responsiveness, and do not set limits. Parents are unsupportive of their children, but will still provide basic needs for the child. Neglectful parents are focused on their own needs more than the needs of their own child. As infants, children have a disturbed attachment with parents, characterised by confusion because the infant does not have a consistent way of coping with the neglect.

Children whose parents are neglectful develop the sense that other aspects of the parents' lives are more important than they are. Children often display contradictory behaviour, and are emotionally withdrawn from social situations. This disturbed attachment also impacts relationships later on in life. These children tend to be socially incompetent. They frequently have low self-esteem, are immature, and may be alienated from the family. In adolescence, they may show patterns of truancy and delinquency.

Children of neglectful parenting exhibit antisocial behaviour as a teenager towards friends and family. They often experience depression and social withdrawal, and are more likely to engage in risky sexual behaviour and drugs than children of authoritative parents. Many times children will grow up feeling resentment against their parents for being neglectful and often might be estranged from them into adulthood.

Attachment Parenting

Attachment parenting, a phrase coined by pediatrician William Sears, is a parenting philosophy based on the principles of the attachment theory in developmental psychology. According to attachment theory, the child forms a strong emotional bond with caregivers during childhood with lifelong consequences. Sensitive and emotionally available parenting helps the child to form a secure attachment style which fosters a child's socioemotional development and well-being. Less sensitive and emotionally available parenting or neglect of the child's needs may result in insecure forms of attachment style, which is a risk factor for many mental health problems. In extreme and rare conditions the child may not form an attachment at all and may suffer from reactive attachment disorder. Principles of attachment parenting aim to increase development of child's secure attachment and decrease insecure attachment.

Although there is research which shows that when mothers are taught to increase their sensitivity to an infant's needs and signals, this increases the development of the child's attachment security, there are no conclusive empirical efficacy studies on Sears attachment parenting.

Attachment theory, originally proposed by John Bowlby, states that the infant has a tendency to seek closeness to another person and feel secure when that person is present. Bowlby had earlier proposed in his maternal deprivation hypothesis that maternal deprivation would not only cause depression in children, but also acute conflict and hostility, decreasing their ability to form healthy relationships in adult life.

In comparison, Sigmund Freud proposed that attachment was a consequence of the need to satisfy various drives. In attachment theory, attachment is considered a biological system and children are naturally attached to their parents because they are social beings, not just because they need other people to satisfy drives.

Developmental psychologist Mary Ainsworth devised a procedure, called The Strange Situation, to observe attachment relationships between a human caregiver and child. She observed disruptions to the parent/child attachment over a 20 minute period, and noted that this affected the child's exploration and behaviour toward the mother. This operationalisation of attachment has recently come under question, as it may not be a valid measure for infants that do not experience distress upon initial encounter with a stranger.

According to Attachment Parenting International (API) there are 8 principles that foster healthy (secure) attachment between the caretaker and infant. While none of these principles is derived directly from original attachment research, they are presented as parenting practices that can lead to "attunement", "consistent and sensitive responsiveness" and "physical and emotional availability" that research has found to be key factors in secure attachment.

Principles of Attachment Parenting

Per Dr. Sears' theory of attachment parenting (AP), proponents such as the API attempt to foster a secure bond with their children by promoting eight principles which are identified as goals for parents to strive for. These eight principles are:

1. Preparation for pregnancy, birth and parenting.
2. Feed with love and respect.
3. Respond with sensitivity.
4. Use nurturing touch.
5. Ensure safe sleep, physically and emotionally.

6. Provide consistent loving care.
7. Practice positive discipline.
8. Strive for balance in personal and family life.

These values are interpreted in a variety of ways. Many attachment parents also choose to live a natural family living (NFL) lifestyle, such as natural childbirth, home birth, stay-at-home parenting, co-sleeping, breastfeeding, baby-wearing, home-schooling, un-schooling, the anti-circumcision movement, natural health, cooperative movements, naturism and support of organic and local foods. However, Dr. Sears does not require a parent to strictly follow any set of rules, instead encouraging parents to be creative in responding to their child's needs. Attachment parenting, outside the guise of Dr. Sears, focuses on responses that support secure attachments.

Childcare

Attachment parenting proponents value secure attachment between children and a primary caregiver, preferably a parent or guardian. Secure primary or secondary attachments may also be formed with other caregiving adults and should be supported by the parents. Even when engaging non-parental caregivers, Attachment Parents strive to maintain healthy, secure attachments with their children. AP-friendly childcare is a continuation of the nurturing care given by the parents and focuses on meeting the child's needs. Attachment Parents typically work to make caregiving arrangements that are sensitive to the child while balancing their own needs as well.

Discipline

Attachment parents seek to understand the biological and psychological needs of the children, and to avoid unrealistic expectations of child behaviour. In setting boundaries and limits that are appropriate to the age of the child, attachment parenting takes into account the physical and psychological stage of development that the child is currently experiencing. In this way, parents may seek to avoid frustration that occurs when they expect things beyond the child's capability. Discipline means teaching the child by gentle guidance, such as re-direction, natural consequences, listening and modelling, and not by punitive means such as spanking, time-out, grounding, and punitive consequences.

Attachment parenting holds that it is vital to the survival of the child that he be capable of communicating needs to the adults to have those needs promptly met. Dr. Sears advises that, while still an infant, the child is mentally incapable of outright manipulation. Unmet needs are believed, by Dr. Sears and other AP proponents, to surface beginning immediately in attempts to fulfil that which was left unmet. AP looks at child development as well as infant and child biology to determine the psychologically and biologically appropriate response at different stages. Attachment parenting does not mean meeting a need that a child can fulfil himself. It means understanding what the needs are, when they arise, how they change over time and circumstances, and being flexible in devising ways to respond appropriately.

Concerted Cultivation

Concerted cultivation is a style of parenting that is marked by a parent's attempts to foster their child's talents through organised leisure activities. This parenting style is commonly exhibited in middle and upper class families. Many have attributed cultural benefits to this form of child-rearing due to the style's use in higher income families, conversely affecting the social habitus of children raised in such a manner. A child that has been concertedly cultivated will often express greater social prowess in social situations involving formality or structure attributed to their increased experience in organised clubs, sports, musical groups as well as increased experience with adults and power structure. While this pattern of child rearing holds no innate positive qualities it has been linked to increased financial and academic success.

Negative considerations have included an overburdened sense of entitlement, lack of creativity, and the psychosomatic inability to play or relax, so advocates of Slow parenting prefer less management of childhood activities. None of these effects can be considered without broader cultural and economic considerations. Concerted cultivation also emphasises the use of reasoning skills and variations in language use. Parents start to encourage their children to learn how to speak with adults so that they become comfortable and understand the importance of eye contact and speaking properly at an earlier age. Concerted cultivation causes a transmission of differential advantages, meaning they end up having an advantage in life over children reared based on other methods. Children who are reared using the concerted cultivation method are set apart in academic environments and they also learn to have more confidence when confronted with social interactions.

Children start to form a certain sense of entitlement because of their early comfort with interacting with adults. Children also become more comfortable questioning adults and it is easier for them to see themselves as equals. With concerted cultivation, the practices often infiltrate into the family life. Frequent gatherings provide opportunities for further cultivation such as eating at the dinner table together.

OVERPARENTING

Parents who try to involve themselves in every aspect of their child's life, often attempting to solve all their problems. A helicopter parent is a colloquial, early 21st-century term for a parent who pays extremely close attention to his or her children's experiences and problems, and attempts to sweep all obstacles out of their paths, particularly at educational institutions. Helicopter parents are so named because, like helicopters, they hover closely overhead. It is a form of overparenting.

Some educationists are now referring to "Lawnmower parents" to describe mothers and fathers who attempt to smooth out and mow down all obstacles, to the extent that they may even attempt to interfere at their children's workplaces, regarding salaries and promotions, after they have graduated from college and are supposedly living on their own. As the children of "helicopter parents" graduate and move into the job market, personnel and human resources departments are becoming acquainted with the phenomenon as well. Some have reported that parents have even begun intruding on salary negotiations. An extension of the term, "Black Hawk parents," has been coined for those who cross the line from a mere excess of zeal to unethical behaviour, such as writing their children's college admission essays.

Risk management is a key skill for everybody, but which some children are denied; helicopter parents often restrict their children's activities. Alongside the constant supervision of children is extreme risk aversion and a disproportionate paranoia about risks covered in media reports such as paedophilia. Children are encouraged to spend more time indoors, for example, watching television, instead of exploring outdoors. The longer-term risks of these practises, such as obesity, bad health and poor risk assessment are accepted because of the perceived child protection advantages. It also deepens generational segregation, encouraging children to view adults as potential abusers.

Institutions such as schools often follow similar risk-averse principles, keeping children in the classroom for more time and forbidding even those activities previously considered a normal part of life. In the longer-term, the children remain inexperienced both in dealing with the real world, and in making decisions.

Nurturant Parenting

The nurturant parent model envisions a family model where children are expected to explore their surroundings with protection from their parents. This model believes that children inherently know what they need and should be allowed to explore. The parents are responsible for protecting their child during this exploration, including protecting their child from themselves by offering guidance. A child will be picked up if the child cries because the parent wants the child to feel safe and nurtured. If a child grows up believing that its needs will be met, it will be more confident when facing challenges.

Ideas involved in this model include:

- True discipline is not a matter of strict obedience, but of respect and compassion.
- The world is no more inherently hostile than it is inherently friendly; it merely commands respect.
- Respect and compassion can only be taught by example.

The nurturant parent model is discussed by George Lakoff in his books, including *Moral Politics and Whose Freedom*? Lakoff argues that if the metaphor of nation as family and government as parent is used, then progressive politics correspond to the nurturant parent model. For example, progressives want the government to make sure that the citizens are protected and assisted to achieve their potential. This might take the form of tough environmental regulations or healthcare assistance.

Slow Parenting

Slow parenting is a parenting style of fewer organised activities for children, instead allowing them to enjoy their childhood and explore the world at their own pace. It is a response to Concerted cultivation and the widespread trend for parents to schedule activities and classes after school every day and every weekend, to solve problems on behalf of the children, and to buy services from commercial suppliers rather than letting nature take its course.

Goals

Slow parenting aims for the goal of allowing children to be happy and satisfied with their own achievements, even though this may not make them the wealthiest or most famous. Since parents will inevitably invest time, money and effort in parenting, they may expect a direct return on that investment.

The parents of modern children are often encouraged to give each child the best possible childhood experiences, to ensure their success and happiness in adult life. However, this often leads to over-stressed children who do not know how to take care of themselves. Their imagination and attention span are reduced. They expect constant stimulation. They are unable to cope with the unpredictability of the real world, either expecting their helicopter parents to intervene, or complaining about unfairness. They may not even understand who they are themselves until much later in adulthood.

Play

Play is the best way of allowing children to explore and discover at their own pace. Children invest 15 per cent of their energy in playing demonstrating their natural inclination and evolutionary benefit. Other mammals also play in developing their own skills in a realistic but less dangerous environment. However, toys, technology and an adult-imposed educational curriculum are not required. Formal learning is more beneficial from the age of six.

Nature

Throughout each interpretation of slow parenting, the natural world is repeatedly emphasised as an under-used resource. Simply letting children out to play in the garden, or wherever they may find, is recommended. For more carefully considered natural experiences, especially for pre-school-age children, forest kindergartens offer people with educational and supervision experience to watch children while they play in a woodland.

Access to nature is often denied to modern children because it conflicts with several modern issues, as discussed below. There may be unfamiliar people in a public park, presenting Stranger danger. There may be risks of personal injury, for example, by walking into the branch of a tree, falling from a height or twisting an ankle on uneven ground. It less supervised, meaning that helicopter parents won't find it so easy to monitor what their children are doing. It is free, and therefore not encouraged by the commercial interests that influence us.

Toys

Any complex toys, even "educational" ones, limit opportunities for exploration because they already have an agenda programmed in to their design. This is particularly true of modern branded toys which are often designed to be limited, or to follow a narrative from a specific story.

Electronic toys have designs which may surpress the child's imagination and limit exploration of both the world and the objects in front of them. A simple toy such as a wooden stick would require the child to imagine what it represents, would be almost infinitely flexible in its use, and would last much longer.

Parents sometimes guide children quite explicitly in their use of toys. For example, showing them which jigsaw puzzle piece they should take next, or demonstrating the features of the latest purchase. Slow parenting would recommend that the parent stand back and let the child decide what to try. Completing the jigsaw, or getting the high score, should not be the main purpose. A helicopter parent may constantly guide their child to the "right" solution. Buying expensive toys as a substitute for spending time with children is a familiar and ineffective parenting choice.

Television

Television is not interactive; a person can watch it with little thinking and without acting. It can occupy an enormous amount of time, and is very explicit. At the same time, it is often created by commercial interests with minimal investment in the programme content and a maximum of advertising. The Social aspects of television are widely discussed and often considered to be negative. Introducing children, including families watching it together to this is a recommendation to continue this lifestyle, and a discouragement to any other play or activity.

TV advertisements often encourage people further into consumerism by promoting expensive objects which are often unnecessary and ultimately unsatisfying (a satisfied customer may not need to make further purchases). The presentation of these to people who are tired or not concentrating is a further risk to their behavioural development. However, it is recognised that television is a convenient baby-sitter, and that some programmes are enjoyable. Each family can make its own choice. These might include watching only ten year old pre-recorded video tapes, or watching broadcast TV with children and giving a real-time commentary on the content and its message.

After-school Classes

Many modern parents feel under pressure to send their children to after-school activities every day of the week. Football, drama, tennis, swimming and art classes develop skills which are widely encouraged. However, the benefits of these activities are less clear.

Cramming schools and private tutors push children to achieve higher academic results, for example in mathematics or literacy, than they would simply at school, but with debatable success; the countries with the most successful schooling start when then children are older, and spend fewer hours at school. Excluding other activities, and making children exhausted every evening, bears an often-forgotten cost. Even school homework is of questionable value, by comparison to the opportunity cost of missing out on other activities.

Some of the classes are motivated by a culture of frequent examinations. Getting in to the right high school or university may depend on results, and studying until 9 p.m. most nights may be seen by parents as the way to achieve it. Some schools formally evaluate the performance of children, even at primary age, putting the children under continuous competitive pressure.

All of these activities are directed by adults, and so children are again prevented from following their own path of discovery and development. These activities have three consequences, in addition to whatever direct benefit they may (or may not) achieve.

- The time spent in classes, and spent travelling to and from each venue (typically by car) cannot be used for other activities. They cannot play at their friends' houses nor look for snails in the garden.
- Adult-organised activities reduce the child's opportunity for creativity and independence.
- The financial cost of classes to parents is often non-trivial.

Support for after-school activities is often in terms of childcare to fill the hours between school and when parents return from work. Amongst those young people who end up with teenage pregnancies or taking drugs, delinquency peaks at around 4. p.m. on school days. The benefit for children less at risk of such outcomes is less clear.

Risk Aversion

As most families have fewer children now than they would have 100 years ago, they invest more in the well-being of each child, and wish to protect that investment. Unfortunately this leads to parents stopping children from facing risks. Rather than let the child work out how to handle it, they make the decision on their behalf. When they deem an activity to be at all risky, some parents withdraw the children completely. Everyday life does contain risk, and in order to develop a healthy understanding of that, children must be allowed to face risks. This means that, from time to time, they may suffer from the materialisation of a risk.

Because many parents have now been raised themselves in a risk-averse way, they are often unable to manage their own situation, and unable to judge which risks are serious. For example, stranger danger, a cornerstone of child safety, has been criticised because it assumes that all strangers are dangerous, and all familiar people are safe. In fact, only a tiny number of abductions by strangers occur in the India each year; far fewer than the number perpetrated by people known to the child.

Family

Spending time with children is always recommended for parents. The book *The Price of Privilege* finds that eating dinner together as a family is an indicator of good psychological health. Tom Hodgkinson's ideal scenario is to be near his children, although not too near.

Strict Parenting

The strict father model of parenting is one which places strong value on discipline as a means to survive and thrive in a harsh world. Ideas involved in this model include:

- That children learn through reward and punishment, as in operant conditioning.
- That children become more self-reliant and more self-disciplined by having strict parents.
- That the parent, particularly the father, is meant to mete out rewards for good behaviour as well as punish bad behaviour.

So this model of child-rearing would involve allowing a child to cry themselves to sleep. Picking up a child when it should be sleeping might foster dependence on the parents and is not a display of discipline. In his book *Dare to Discipline,* James Dobson advocates the strict father model. However, researchers have linked authoritarian child-rearing with children who withdraw, lack spontaneity, and have lesser evidence of conscience.

Parenting for Everyone

The philosophy of Parenting For Everyone (PEE) was created by Simon Soloveychik and expressed in his book *Parenting For Everyone*. According to Soloveychik:

> "Not many of us can love children, even our own children. Not many of us are wise enough to control our own behaviour. Not many of us can avoid anger and be in command of ourselves. In most cases we are tired and irritated. But children soften our hearts—by their existence, by their laughing and pranks. We just have to be brave. We must not fear kindness in our hearts or be afraid of "what if something wrong happens!" We cannot become better than we are; we cannot become stronger than we are; we cannot love more than we do; we cannot change our will or character, but we can change our vision of a child, our imagination about him, the image of a Child, and we can gradually form another, new, better attitude toward him. Here is my chance. This is the only chance for a weak, incapable, and imperfect parent."

PFE is a comprehensive book on parenting, which is unlike any other book on the market discusses parenting from a different perspective, from perspective of ethics. PFE discusses in depth the goals, conditions and means of upbringing. It continues by going into detail about upbringing the heart, spirit and intelligence of a child through communication, cooperation, and co-creativity.

The basic premise of PFE is the "foundation of the good life of a man is being conscientious and kind." The author strongly believed that kindness is the key to raising good children. According to the author there must be at least one person in a child's life who sets a good example for a child, showing kindness to the child. What matters most is that someone in the child's life "sincerely and deeply, and without hesitation believes in kindness and honesty, or in love and conscience". This premise has been touted by child psychologists and other how-to authors of parenting books.

Raising a kind child is done by allowing the child to be kind. People teach children about freedom by letting them be free, teach responsibility by letting them be responsible, teach goodness and conscience through goodness and conscience, and people teach children to be happy by being happy, because 'we raise not a child but a man".

There are three major precepts that come up again and again in this book: truth, goodness and beauty. The truth is that there is a definite line between good and evil; people generally know this and accept it. This knowing and acceptance is called intelligence. For a child/man to be a complete human means that person's heart, spirit, and intelligence needs to be developed. The truth about a man is that man is created for goodness, for infinitely increasing dignity. People are free when they learn the truth about themselves.

Taking Children Seriously

Taking Children Seriously (TCS) is a parenting movement and educational philosophy whose central idea is that is possible and desirable to raise and educate children without either doing anything to them against their will, or making them do anything against their will.

TCS begins with the observation that most traditional interactions between adults and youth are based on coercion. The TCS model of parenting and education rejects this coercion as infringing on the will of the child, and also rejects parental or educator "self-sacrifice" as infringing on the will of the adult. TCS advocates that parents and children work to find a common preference, a solution all parties genuinely prefer to all other candidate solutions they can think of.

The TCS philosophy was inspired by the epistemology of Karl Popper. Popper was a professional educator himself before he started to do philosophy. In fact, philosophy was only a second option for him at that time, to be able to emigrate to escape the imminent Anschluss.

Outcomes of Parenting

Research into the child behaviour outcomes associated with each type of parenting has traditionally shown a strong benefit to authoritative parenting. These children have been shown to have more self-discipline, emotional self-control, more friends and better school performance. However, recent research has identified a number of caveats.

First, authoritarian parenting may be more effective in certain contexts and in social groups other than those studied in early research.

Secondly, little research has examined the genetic influences that may underlie the findings. For instance, harsh parents may produce harsher children through the mechanism of genetic transmission of these traits. Behaviour genetics research is currently examining the influence of genes as they pertain to parenting styles.

An additional criticism of the parenting styles research is that parenting has been shown to be part of a bi-directional relationship between parent and child. Thus, characterising a parenting style as arising from the parent leaves out the essential influence of the child on the parent-child dyad.

3

Prenatal Parenting

Becoming a father/mother is one of most beautiful aspects of human life. When a women become pregnant, a new life takes shape within her, is molded and then is born to be nurtured into a good human being. There are women who recall the ordeal of pregnancy, but yet none would deny it is a blessing to be able to give birth. Like some mothers would say, it is a sweet ordeal to feel the little one grow and develop through the nine months. It is a sweet kind of pain when the fetus within kicks the mother to move about. There is something pleasant about the morning sickness, knowing that there is a little being forming in there. All this is part of the process known as prenatal parenting.

In our society, the majority opinion is that parenthood starts after birth. This view has been fostered by medical scientists who define a baby as physical matter, especially brain matter, which they have long believed is insufficient to register or process memory, learning, trauma, emotion, or any truly human experiences until months after birth. This effectively excludes the period of life in the womb from active parenting. Hence, we have a cultural delusion that "early" parenting begins after a child is born.

Considering all we know today about the realities of life before birth, we must reset the clock on parenthood.

To start parenting *early,* you cannot miss the period from conception to birth! All the new facts of life plead for parental involvement and participation in the powerful matrix of intimate interactions that take place in the womb. Pregnancy is parenting *de facto.* Parental influence on a child is at its peak during construction *in utero.* Creating is what early parenting is about—creating a physical body and brain, creating emotional foundations for living, and establishing a rich connection with the prenatal self.

A growing group of modern parents appreciate that their own health, habits, and environment will determine the quality of their conception and they know their efforts at "quality control" can spare their baby from a lifetime of sickness and handicap. They are not alone in realising that with habitual use, alcohol, drugs, and tobacco are teratogens which can create birth defects. For example, when fathers are cigarette smokers, they damage their sperm and pass to their offspring a higher risk of childhood cancer. Experts estimate that as many as 15 per cent of childhood cancers could be due to smoking by fathers. The cancer risk is proportional to the number of cigarettes smoked per day. Parent smoking also plays a role in sudden infant death syndrome and in production of smaller babies. How many mothers and fathers would deliberately create cancer in their children if they knew how to avoid it?

Bad timing can have unforseen results. For example, if mothers consume alcohol at the time of conception, they raise the risk of giving birth to babies with facial anomalies (and having to look at these anomalies for a lifetime). To avoid other birth defects, couples preparing for a conscious (rather than unconscious) conception may want to rid themselves of heavy metals, eliminate the need for multiple prescriptions, or fortify themselves nutritionally before bringing egg and sperm together.

Having sufficient folic acid in the system before conception may insure normal development of the neural tube, protecting their child from *spina bifida* and anencephaly. Chronic occupational stress can lower fertility rates, preventing parenting altogether. When it doesn't, an unplanned conception may provide a stiff challenge to the baby who must continually swim in a sea of discontent that is not their fault!

Health risks aside, some parents today are being startled by encounters with babies before they have been conceived. These parents are drawn into very early parenting by vivid dreams, visions, and appearances that come weeks, months, or even years in advance of physical conception.

Today most couples prefer the process known as a planned pregnancy, because of various factors; prime amongst them being the financial well being to support the birth and nurturing of a child. In such cases, the first prenatal visit actually happens prior to actual pregnancy, to see whether one is ready to go off the contraception pills and conceive a baby. However, in maximum conceptions, one is unaware of the pregnancy until actual realisation dawns after one skips the first menstrual cycle. Normally doctors except ladies to pay their first visit anywhere between the sixth and twelfth week after conception.

Apart from all the physical care required to ensure the healthy development of the fetus, the mother actual starts proper parenting during pregnancy. Like they say, the permanent impressions of a human being are imprinted on the mind while in the womb of the mother. So, just as the food she eats determines the bodily development of the child; the kind of feelings and thoughts and words she fills herself with and exchanges with others affect the child's mental and emotional development.

Creating a Physical Body

Parents provide the immediate physical environment which will determine whether the baby's equipment for living will be poor, average, or optimal. As the foundations for physical life are laid, each new part is built upon the previous one so that both limitations and advantages are preserved. Although some degree of "plasticity" is possible during later development, the original parts remain in place.

Parents who wait to think about this until after their child is born will be starting too late—nine months after all the basic equipment has been constructed. In the 20th century, parents began to face compounding hazards of reproduction. These included old and new bacteria and viruses, which seem to emerge when our immune system is weak and vulnerable. In addition, environmental dangers became more challenging with the huge new production of industrial and agricultural chemicals, a swelling tide of stimulants and sedatives such as nicotine, caffein, and alcohol, tempting "street" drugs like opiates and amphetamines, the plethora of new drugs prescribed by physicians, new forms of electromagnetic radiation including the bombardment of ultrasound waves being overused to entertain parents during obstetrical office visits. Because of so much environmental disruption, the safety and sanctity of the womb is threatened as never before.

A mother's diet can innocently invite birth defects. Science has only slowly found the connection between deficiencies of folic acid (one of the B vitamins) and the profound malformations of anencephaly and spina bifida, defects which occur when the neural tube fails to close 18 to 26 days after conception. If construction deficits occur at the top end of the tube, the baby's brain will likely be affected; if at the lower end, the spinal column will likely be affected. Large scale disruptions in the food supply, as in a famine, can create widespread problems of reproduction. Long-term studies of children born to mothers who were starved in early pregnancy show damage to the mechanisms of appetite control and growth regulation, resulting in obesity in the offspring. Famines produce increased rates of diabetes and schizophrenia, partly through zinc deficiency which contributes to both of these diseases. Sub-optimal nutrition, one of the factors behind the plague of low-weight babies, means shortages of essential supplies during brain construction resulting in a sub-optimal brain. In the modern urban environment, estrogenic compounds flow freely and have an impact on human sexual development. Hormonal deficiencies, excesses, and imbalances effect both the genes and the environment that ultimately determine sexual identity and orientation—all this before the baby is born.

Creating Emotional Foundations

One of the biggest surprises about life in the womb is the extent of emotional involvement and expression, generally not anticipated in psychology or medicine. Spontaneous and graceful movement that can now be observed from about 10 weeks after conception reveals self-expression and early aspects of self-control, needs and interests. Some behaviours reflect a protest against uncomfortable experiences. By 15 weeks, ultrasound shows babies moving in reaction to something as simple as a mother's laugh or cough. More disturbing are the aggressive actions seen toward the needle during amniocentesis—attacking the needle barrel with a closed fist, suggesting self-protection, self-assertion, fear and anger that was previously thought unreal and impossible.

With surprising development of hearing and tasting before 16 weeks gestational age, the way is open for babies to have even more extensive interactions with their mothers and fathers. Ultrasound imaging of twins similarly shows the unexpected scope of their social relationships seen in repeated hitting, kicking, kissing, or playing together. Life in the womb—now that we can observe it—bears little resemblance to the lazy world previously hypothesised in which a baby was a passive passenger virtually deaf, dumb, and blind. In those days, parents themselves thought it was appropriate to be deaf, dumb, and blind.

As it is with the establishment of physical settings in utero, the emotional system is also organising itself in relation to the range and varieties of experiences encountered. A baby surrounded with anger, fear, and anxiety will adjust itself to that world and probably carry those settings into life. Patterns of fearful reaction already visible via ultrasound before birth are repeated after birth. This emotional sensitivity of the fetus is one big reason why adoption cannot be viewed as just an experience for the parents. Chances are, an adopted baby has emerged from confusion and conflict, both troubled and conditioned by the turmoil of the birth parents. They have been learning from experience and are likely to arrive feeling upset and rejected, carrying unconscious baggage of anxiety about its identity and connections. Parents are very real participants in this dynamic world of the unborn.

Establishing Relation with the Prenate

Not long ago we thought it was impossible for prenates to have any truly personal or significant experiences. We didn't see that they could have a working mind. In retrospect, our false beliefs about their brain power obscured the fact that babies in the uterine world were indeed having potentially rich experiences, establishing patterns of interaction, listening to music and conversation, and as tests ultimately proved, were committing them to memory. Numerous experiments have made it clear that prenates who have the opportunity to hear stories and music repeated to them in utero can demonstrate recognition for this material later in life. Prenates have become familiar with and show a preference for specific lullabies, musical themes like "Peter and the Wolf," "Mary had a little Lamb," and even theme music from television soap operas.

Prenates memorise the voices of their mothers and fathers in utero while learning the basic features of their native language, the "mother tongue" as we say. Spectrographic analysis of voice and cry sounds as early as 26 weeks of gestation show how far babies of this age have already progressed in adopting the voice characteristics of the mother. In a recent experiment, mothers repeated a children's rhyme daily for four weeks from week 33 to 37 in utero. Tested at 37 weeks while still inside, the babies reacted with a change of heartbeat to the familiar rhyme, but not to the unfamiliar rhyme. In other research, babies have demonstrated immediately after birth a preference for their mother's voice and their native language. The womb turns out to be a stimulating place and is, in many ways, a school.

In the last fifteen years as these facts were gradually becoming known, many books, tapes, and exercises were created to help parents understand and communicate with babies in the womb. All are potentially valuable in helping parents to make a creative and loving attachment, a connection which respects the needs and limitations of the baby. Babies are naturally curious and interactive. There is no need for pushing and shoving.

Since about 1980, organised programmes for parents have been developed and tested, revealing the benefits of carefully planned stimulation. By 1990, programmes with sophisticated experimental designs and systematic testing were underway. The largest experiment in prenatal stimulation has taken place in Caracas, Venezuela under the direction of psychologist Beatriz Manrique, where six hundred families have been involved in an experiment which tested the babies for six years following their prenatal programme. Test results revealed the advantages of prenatal stimulation in virtually every category over the entire time period including verification of superior auditory and speech development, motor skills, memory, and intelligence.

Prenatal Development

One of the most beautiful phases during a woman's lifetime is the nine-month pregnancy tenure. Yes, there are ups and downs that do occur during this period; but all that is done away when one thinks of the little life that is taking its form within the womb. This is what makes womanhood so special—the possibility of motherhood. And to ensure healthy pregnancy tenure one needs to follow every recommended step and procedure that is prescribed to bring about consistent prenatal development.

The mother-to-be is required to go through prenatal testing from time-to-time. This is an essential as the various tests monitor the growth and development of the fetus, thereby ruling out any complications, as well as bringing under control any possible damage or harm that could have been accidentally done to the fetus. Thus, the prenatal tests are essential for the following reasons:

1. It helps to identify any kind of health problems a mother-to-be faces, in order to see that the child is not affected.
2. It helps to find out about various characteristics of the fetus such as the size, gender, age and most importantly the placement of the uterus during the pregnancy period.

3. The tests help check whether the fetus is developing or has developed any congenital, genetic or chromosomal troubles

4. The tests monitor any types of fetal abnormalities such as organ development, as well as heart related malfunctioning.

One of the important tests is the prenatal ultrasound. This is a video test of the fetus. The test helps monitor the healthy growth and development of the fetus, especially checking the heart functioning and over all body development that is supposed to happen in accordance to trimester charts.

The pregnancy development stages are divided into three trimesters. The gynecologists and obstetricians have standardised charts and timetables according to which they can monitor whether the fetus is developing healthily or not. There is a an average growth and development that happens during each trimester, if the fetus is developing and growing within the normal averages prescribed then there is no reason for concern. However, in case of any abnormalities, it can be controlled by the development monitoring.

Apart from the battery of tests, the mother-to-be is required to follow a proper diet for a healthy pregnancy. The prescribed diet has to be rich in all essential nutrients, yet according to the prescribed requirement-level. One needs to ensure that one consumes a balanced diet and visit the nutritionist or dietician regularly to have the diet changed as per requirement. One needs to be aware that as the fetus is growing and developing, the needs for its good health also keep changing. So, there is no nine-month standard diet.

Medical science is constantly making large advancing and progressive steps. The latest development in the field of prenatal tests is the 3D ultrasound prenatal diagnosis.

In this test the obstetrician gets a detailed three-dimensional clipping of the fetus. This helps in closer to perfect diagnosis during pregnancy. And more so it is the most exciting moment for the parents-to-be to see next-to-life video of the fetus within, as it is.

It is very important that one monitors baby development during pregnancy. This will help bring under control any possible complications that could have developed or could possibly develop. And these tests should be conducted and administered during the various stages of pregnancy development. Ideally one should maintain a proper chart or time-table to see that the tests are done periodically. Importantly prenatal diagnosis helps in regulating healthy development of the mother-to-be and human life-to-be.

Understanding the Behaviour of Fetus

Ultrasound technology has provided a window through which the behaviour of the fetus may be observed. Although pregnant women report feeling their baby move at around 16–20 weeks of gestation, ultrasound observations have revealed that the fetus begins to move at 7–8 weeks. These first movements appear slow and originate in the spinal cord: the back may flex or extend, and this results in passive movements of the arms and legs. The types of movement exhibited by the fetus expand rapidly and by 14–15 weeks virtually all the movements the fetus will exhibit have emerged. As the fetus develops, its movements become organised into periods of activity and inactivity. This culminates at the end of pregnancy with the emergence of four behavioural states—quiet sleep, active sleep, quiet awake, active awake—precursors of the behavioural states seen in newborns.

The examination of fetal movements has produced some fascinating discoveries. For example, handedness is observed from 10 weeks of gestation. Intriguingly, there have been no reports of hemispheric differences at this age, which may suggest that it is differential left- and right-sided movements that lead to lateralisation of brain function rather than the other way round. Rapid eye movements, associated with dreaming in adults, have been observed in the last third of pregnancy.

Early views of the fetus portrayed its environment as one of sensory deprivation. Research has revised this view and demonstrated that the fetus has considerable sensory abilities. The only sense unlikely to be stimulated naturally in the womb is that of vision, as the mother's clothes and tissue will block out light.

The first sense to develop is that of touch. By eight weeks of gestation the fetus responds to touch around the lips and cheeks. By 14 weeks most of its body, excluding the back and top of the head, responds to touch. The fetus touches its face from 10–11 weeks and contact with the umbilical cord and uterine wall, and possibly other womb mates, provides tactile stimulation.

Flavours from the mother's diet pass into the amniotic fluid, so when the fetus begins to swallow this fluid, around the 12th week of gestation, it may experience the flavours of its mother's diet. By 15–16 weeks the fetus responds to the flavor of the amniotic fluid swallowing more if the fluid tastes sweet but less if it tastes 'bitter'.

The fetus responds to sound from 22–24 weeks. Initially, responses are found only in the low-frequency range (250–500 Hz) of adult hearing (20–20000 Hz), but this range expands as the fetus matures. In late pregnancy, the fetus can discriminate between different voices and speech sounds—'BIBA' and 'BABI'.

The uterine environment of the fetus is quite noisy. The mother's heartbeat, blood flow and digestive system all contribute to the fetus's auditory world. Sounds from the external world can be heard, although with some attenuation by the mother's tissues. Interestingly, there is little attenuation around 125–250 Hz, the fundamental frequency of the human voice. Thus, the mother talking and other speech sounds in the environment will be readily heard and will form a major part of the fetus's environment.

One sensory ability that has aroused considerable interest is that of pain sensation. The determination of whether the fetus feels pain is made more difficult by the fact that pain is a subjective phenomenon. Pain responses have been observed in the premature infant from around 24–26 weeks, a time when the neural pathways for pain are first formed. Biochemical stress responses to needle punctures during blood transfusions are found from 23 weeks. These, however, are all indirect measures of pain, and debate is rife as to whether the fetus feels pain. Although lacking a definitive answer, this does not prevent consideration of the use of analgesia for the fetus and it may be appropriate to err on the side of caution and administer analgesia irrespective of whether the fetus feels pain or not. However, the analgesia itself may have adverse consequences; more research is needed to resolve this issue.

Whether the fetus can learn has attracted considerable interest, possibly because learning is often seen as the pinnacle of adult achievement. Early studies of learning in the 1930s and 1940s, perhaps reflecting the zeitgeist, demonstrated classical conditioning in late pregnancy. Peiper reported a decrement in fetal response to a repeated sound (car horn), and more recently the fetus has been demonstrated to habituate to auditory stimuli from around 22–24 weeks.

Newborns prefer their mother's voice to that of an unfamiliar female, a preference that is acquired prenatally. Newborns prefer music they have heard prenatally to that which they have never heard. Interestingly, this preference can be observed at 36 weeks but not 30 weeks, which may indicate that learning of familiar sounds or tunes occurs after 30 weeks.

The fetus also learns about tastes and smells. For example, if the mother eats garlic during her pregnancy her newborn exhibits less of an aversion to garlic than newborns whose mothers did not eat garlic. Newborns show a preference for the odour of their mother over that of another female and orient to their own amniotic fluid, both observations suggestive of prenatal learning of odours and tastes. Whether long-term preferences can result from prenatal learning is unknown. Newborn preferences for music acquired prenatally disappear by three weeks of age in the absence of any postnatal exposure.

The fetus is continually active in and reactive to its environment. Researches suggest the behaviour of the fetus is important for its development both before and after birth, ensuring its survival and beginning its integration into the social world.

Improving Fetal Well-being

As more knowledge is gained about the behaviour of the fetus and the factors that influence development, opportunities are presented to use this to enhance the health of the fetus. Despite a number of techniques to assess fetal well-being (e.g. analysis of genetic/chromosomal constitution, structure, and autonomic function), none directly assess the functioning of the brain. Since the behaviour of the fetus directly represents the functioning of its nervous system, observation of the fetus's behaviour provides an excellent means of assessing neural function and dysfunction.

Aberrant patterns of behaviour have been observed in fetuses with chromosomal abnormalities, neural tube defects, maternal illness and those exposed to illegal and social drugs. Moreover, analysis of behaviour enables the severity of effect to be determined. Examining the behaviour of the fetus has advantages when assessing the effects of drugs or potential teratogens. As behaviour reflects the output of the brain, it can provide an assessment of function independent of information on input, which may be difficult to obtain. Assessing behaviour examines the actual effect exposure to alcohol, or other substances, has had on brain function. Although only at the very early stages of development, analysis of the fetus's behaviour may provide important information on fetal health, leading to improved diagnosis and better treatments.

The action of drugs (e.g. thalidomide) on the fetus demonstrates that prenatal influences exert a long-term effect. Recently the role of experiences in influencing the development and function of physiological systems has been recognised, suggesting certain adult diseases have fetal origins—the fetal origins of adult disease hypothesis. Evidence is now accumulating that maternal psychological factors may influence the fetal environment exerting a long-term influence on the developing fetus. This research poses significant challenges for our treatment of the prenatal period.

Recent evidence has suggested an important link between maternal anxiety during pregnancy and outcome after birth. High prenatal maternal anxiety levels have been linked with lower mental and motor development at eight months of age, lower mental development at two years and higher levels of behavioural and emotional problems at six years nine months. It is argued that maternal anxiety influences the functioning of the maternal hypothalamic-pituitary-adrenal axis, which in turn influences fetal brain development, resulting in the subsequent poorer psychological and behavioural performance. This poses major challenges for the public health agenda.

Considerable resources have been employed in attempts to reduce the consumption of alcohol and smoking by pregnant women. What could or should be done to reduce maternal anxiety if this effect on brain development and performance is further confirmed? There is no easy answer, and it is obvious that the scale of any such intervention would be huge and complicated. But this should not mean that the opportunity to enhance development should be ignored.

The first 38 weeks of our development has been shrouded in mystery, but now the embryonic science of fetal psychology is revealing the importance of this period for the rest of our lives. As well as advancing our knowledge of the ontogenetic processes before birth, the greater understanding of prenatal development presents an opportunity to promote the health and well-being of the fetus and provide individuals with the best start in life possible.

Garbh Sanskar

A child's rearing and development begins from the time it is conceived, rather than once it is born. In fact, all the basics of life are learnt through the pregnant mother. Her joys and suffering, her food and exercise, her thoughts and emotions, everything has an impact on the fetus. That is why since time immemorial they say that a mother during pregnancy must devote her time in spiritual/religious practices.

She should be kept happy and healthy. Before feeding the family, she should be well fed. She should surround herself by all that is positive. She must rest well, and exercise sensibly. Her sadness and sorrow, her pain and misery can affect the growth and development of the fetus. And moreover, the fetus is registering every experience the mother is going through.

All this is not just a part of Indian mythology and garbh sanskar, but even today's medical research affirms whatever pregnant ladies would be told eras ago. Today, mothers-to-be, visiting their gynecologists are constantly reminded to keep themselves busy and their minds active, free of anything negative. They are encouraged to practice Yoga and Meditation, in order to bring calm and peace to the mind under all circumstances. In fact, educationists encourage those pregnant to read a lot of educative and value-building books, as well as listen to music that has happy and calming tunes. Some mothers-to-be in fact enjoy listening to enacted fairy tales and nursery rhymes in order to refresh their memories. And this also makes them very happy.

According to a famous tale in Indian Mythology, during the historic battle of Kurushetra, Arjuna's son could courageously take up the challenge of entering the Chakravyu, which was a dangerous spiral plan laid by the enemy camp, because when his mother was pregnant she heard how the entire layout was. However, since she never heard the way of getting out of it, Arjuna's son was killed on the battlefield. Thus, according to this tale, a child learns and recalls even what is heard while in the womb.

Parenting in India, has always been value based. For every family, the most important education for the child is the sanskars and values. Essentially, sanskaars mean 'impressions'. This implies the impressions in the mind that are inculcated because of teachings and experience; and these are fed into the fetal mind and continue to build up throughout life. Thus, the impressions and values are the basis of molding a fetus into a good human being, after which everything follows.

There is a misconception that states that Indian Mythology is religion based. However, this is not true. The entire pantheon of this countries mythology contains interesting tales that are nonetheless exaggerations of reality; but all the same contain practical lessons of life. After all, the human mind enjoys registering all that has an animated story with action and thrill. And this is the essence of each mythological tale. And yet, each story has something special to teach one. There are numerous tales that help those pregnant through their entire term, inducing important values and lessons in parenting. And these tales provide value-based education during the child's formative years.

An essential part of fetal development is something known as *garbh sanskar*. This implies impressions created in the womb. To explain this further, according to not only ancient scriptures, but also modern day scientific researches, the fetus in the womb registers everything that the mother goes through—mental, emotional, physical, etc.,—it registers everything in the form of impressions that also form the basis of life. The fetus registers what makes the mother happy, and what brings her unhappiness. It is for this reason that various music companies have produced audio discs and cassettes that calm the mind and bring a feeling of harmony.

Thus, a pregnant one should remember that the true education is character building that begins with conception and continues through the entire pregnancy period. Once out of the womb, the life begins for the child where learning is about concrete concepts and experiences. However, it has been proven that the foundation of the human character is laid in the womb, through the pregnancy tenure.

For those looking out for various interesting tales to read during pregnancy, one could read about the role of Manu in Indian Mythology. He is considered to be the first man, who was self-created. He is considered to have penned the code of values for human beings, which is an interesting and educative read for the entire family. Apart from this there are numerous Indian fables. The way they have been written is entertaining and actually create animated pictures in the mind, making one a witness of all that is narrated.

Prenatal Yoga

Yoga is a form of exercise that originated in India years ago, but has gained popularity in the nation only in recent times, after it has been popularised in the western world. This is a sad but true fact, that anything to be accepted in India needs to be popular in the west. But all the same, thankfully an increasing number of people are adopting prenatal yoga a healthy way of taking care of oneself through the pregnancy tenure, thereby ensuring the healthy growth and development of the fetus.

There are trained experts, who conduct pre-natal classes in India. These teachers are essentially trained in the various asanas, or postures to help one through the pregnancy, as well as to go through a rather less strenuous labour during childbirth. Apart from the postures one is taught various breathing techniques to relax the mind under all circumstances. This is important because pregnancy can be rather stressful for the mind and body. Because of the irregular hormonal patterns, women complain of mood swings and to add to that is the regular day-to-day stress and tension. This can do a lot of harm not only to the mother, but also the fetus.

Yoga during pregnancy helps fetus to develop healthily. This is because the various stretching postures make for comfortable space for the fetus. And the correct breathing methods ensure complete oxygen flow for the baby forming within. And importantly, it prepares the mother's body for the traumas of labour, strengthening and toning the muscles. Yoga for pregnancy also makes the expectant mother to become more aware of the bodily needs and changes, which maybe pleasant or unpleasant. Through the various breathing techniques taught one can relax the mind, calming it completely while going through a tough phase. After all awareness of the breath helps one to be anchored in the present moment, calming it completely. Even the physical aches, pains and discomfort disappear almost instantly when the mind is at peace.

Today, the popularity of prenatal pregnancy is increasing, with more and more expectant mothers looking out for yoga teachers in this area of specialisation. While most yoga teach yoga postures and breathing techniques for all purposes, yet advisably one should seek experts with certification in fitness prenatal professional yoga. As with the certification one is better equipped to deal with all types of complications that could arise. And those who go through such formal training can also provide an appropriate diet routine to help one go through a healthy pregnancy tenure.

The various prenatal yoga positions help the expectant mother to rid them of the common backache problem they tend to suffer from. Another advantage of practicing yoga is that it actually helps the expectant mother to get back to proper shape soon enough post-pregnancy. As with practice one can actually go through pregnancy without putting on excessive weight; thereby avoiding post-pregnancy crash dieting and rigorous workouts.

Pregnancy classes in India, is becoming a trend in the metro cities, and is slowly and steadily spreading to the smaller cities. However, the fact remains that there are not too many certified teachers in this specific area of yoga. And one is advised to seek an expert with formal certified training to avoid any kind of possible complications. The best option is to find out from one's gynecologist or a maternity hospital or nursing home about any certified prenatal classes in India. Remember, one needs to be sure of the authenticity of the yoga class or teacher, as pregnancy is delicate period and any kind of mis-guidance can lead to unwanted complications.

Prenatal Nutrition

Most couples plan their pregnancy in order to ensure the birth of a healthy baby. Also, nowadays, couples are concerned about their financial status and prefer to plan a pregnancy when they know they are financially stable to not only go through a healthy pregnancy, but also ensure proper education. They want to be sure that they can give their child all the needs and fulfil the wants of their little one.

In order to avoid accidental pregnancy most couples go onto contraceptives and consult with a gynecologist as to when they need to stop birth control measures in order to conceive when they are ready. With such guidance the doctor also suggests certain prenatal vitamins prior to conception to ensure that the body is completely prepared for a new form to take shape in the womb.

Though there are vitamins available in the market, yet most health care specialists suggest that expectant mothers should consume their requirement in the natural form and so they suggest a diet that contains all the nutrients for the healthy growth and development of the fetus, as well as good health of the expectant mother, which is a prime requirement.

Every one of the suggested prenatal vitamins and minerals are essential for the mother-to-be and the being growing and developing within. Sometimes due to aversions and cravings women tend to overlook the need to maintain a daily prenatal food regime, thereby skipping the consumption of the vitamins. Once in a way one can forget to take their routine prescribed in-take, but continuing to do so over a period of time can bring about some dangers to both the mother and child.

Essentially the foods that one consumes should contain folic acid, vitamins and minerals as prescribed by the gynecologist and obstetrician. The following are the various vitamins to take during pregnancy:

1. *Vitamin* C: This is important as it promotes tissue repair, healing of wounds and the bone; and it increases the resistance of the body to infections. It functions as an agent that binds the cells together of the fetus.
2. *Vitamin D:* This helps in general growth by regulating the appropriate calcium and phosphorus; both of which are vital for the development of healthy bones and teeth.
3. *B Vitamins (thiamine, vitamin B6, riboflavin, folic acid)*:
   - *(a) Thiamine* is an agent that converts the carbohydrates to energy in the mother; which in turn is essential for the healthy brain development of the fetus.
   - *(b) Vitamin B6* is important for the development of the fetus' brain and nervous system.
   - *(c) Riboflavin* is important for the growth and development of the fetus' bones, muscles and nervous system.
   - *(d) Folic acid* is one of the B Vitamins, which is essential for the production of red blood cells.

4. *Vitamin A*: This is vital as it promotes the growth of cells, skin and mucous membranes.

The foods one should avoid during pregnancy include soft cheese, unpasteurised milk, caffeine and unwashed fruits and vegetables. And one should compulsorily be aware of the prenatal vitamin rich foods. Ideally, one should seek the guidance of a certified nutritionist in order to be sure that through each trimester one is eating appropriately.

Early pregnancy diet health supplements ensure that the expectant mother is consuming all nutrients in the right balance. However, one should avoid picking up the supplements off the counter and instead seek expert guidance that one is taking the right one. Yet, no supplement can make up for the natural sources of vitamins and other nutrients.

During pregnancy women go through various problems such as brittle nails, excessive hair fall, dryness of hair and skin, or then very oily skin. Gynecologists and obstetricians also consult expectant mothers on prenatal vitamins and hair growth, which seems to be a major worry amongst most women. While they are eager and excited about the birth process, yet they are concerned about the various side effects of pregnancy.

Prenatal Care

In order to ensure the birth of a healthy baby it is necessary for the mother-to-be to maintain holistic good health throughout the pregnancy tenure. It is essential that she take every measure to maintain a healthy body. And in order to maintain a healthy body the mother-to-be needs to follow a proper balanced diet regime that needs to be prescribed by a certified nutritionist and followed up regularly. One needs to also follow a proper exercise routine and take all prescribed medicines. On the mental and emotional level, one should keep oneself happy. No stress, no tension, no sorrow, no misery, no anger, no frustration; only happy and happiness, smiles ad joy, peace and calm. Maintaining holistic good health is a guarantee to giving birth to healthy baby. As much as people consider massages a luxury, it is in fact one of the basic needs of the human body. This is because therapists are trained to massage the body in a way that the muscles and the entire nervous system are relaxed, which automatically relaxes and calms one completely. Prenatal massage has such a therapeutic effect; and more so the therapists are trained to regulate the flow of blood and bring rejuvenation to the tired mind and body.

Due to the constant changes the body is undergoing one needs to keep in check the possibility of swinging towards prenatal depression. This could lead to miscarriage, as well as abnormalities in the growth and development of the fetus. Excessive depression is known to have caused heart and breathing problems in the fetus. And one of the common complications during child birth is the baby getting entangled in the umbilical chord due to a shift in position. According to most gynecologists and obstetricians such shifts are caused by the discomfort the fetus experiences in the womb and tries to shift into a more comfortable position. This discomfort is caused by negative emotions.

Pregnancy and prenatal care go hand-in-hand. One cannot overlook the need for closely monitored prenatal care to be able to bring about the birth of a healthy baby. Today, this is more important than ever before because of the kind of times we are living in. Pollution, stress, worries, troubles, etc., seem to be at an all time high. As much as one is warned to keep stress levels under control, yet it seems almost impossible and this leads to the varied complications, some of which never existed before.

Prenatal care during pregnancy is not only about right eating and exercising, but also regular visits to the doctor and regularly taking the tests in order to monitor if any abnormalities are occurring in the growth and development of the fetus. According to the health care experts one needs to visit the doctor once a month during the first five to six months of pregnancy; every fortnight during the seventh and eighth month and every week in the ninth month.

Prenatal ultrasound of twins needs to be done more regularly than that of the single fetus. This is because the space within the womb is ideally meant for a single baby-growth; and when the twins are forming there is possibility of one dominating over the other and getting more of the nutrition and space. However, constant monitoring, the doctor can ensure that both are growing healthily. Also early detection of any abnormality in one of the twins can prevent it from spreading to the other, especially where infections are concerned.

A more recent advancement in prenatal testing is the 4D prenatal ultrasound imaging. This process provides clearer images of the fetus within and can make out the minutest deformity that otherwise could not be noticed. The images captured seem even more life-like than the other types of ultrasounds. Like they say it is a sleek method of watching the child develop during the periodic checks. This facility is available at most hospitals around the world. Importantly, when going for any type of ultrasound one should remember it is illegal to try and find out the gender of the child, more so in India where female feticide still prevails rampantly even in the metro cities.

4

Parenting of Newborns and Infants

Infants develop in many different ways at the same time. Different aspects of child development are never at rest or waiting for other parts to catch up. Instead, development is simultaneous. While physical growth and maturity are the most obvious signs that development is occurring, children also develop cognitively, socially, emotionally, and sexually.

Development is often described by referring to particular developmental milestones that are significant achievements of one sort or another such as crawling, walking, or first words. Developmental milestones are presented as occurring at particular ages. Even though developmental milestones do commonly occur at particular ages, infants develop at their own pace. Some infants will reach a given milestone early, while others will reach it later on. All of this is perfectly normal.

Coming home from the hospital for the first time with a tiny person who depends entirely on you for all his needs can be a daunting prospect. It's normal for new parents and caregivers to feel a mixture of excitement, joy, and love along with some anxiety, fear, and a little trepidation. However, with some technical and developmental know-how, coupled with the love and support of family friends, time, and patience, new parents can feel like capable professionals.

Holding and Physical Support

In the first two years of life, infants have limited ability to control their movements and to transport themselves around on their own; caregivers have to help them move around their environment as needed and to help them develop their sensory-motor skills to learn to manoeuvre themselves around their environment. When infants are first born, they have little control over their limbs and heads.

Caregivers need to support an infant's body fully as they carry them. When holding young infants, it's important to make sure they are supporting the baby's head and neck in order to stabilise the entire body. Moreover, when caregivers hold their infants securely, they're communicating unconditional love that helps to form the parent-child bond. It is important that when a caregiver holds their baby in the first months of life, they hold them close to their bodies where they will feel warm and safe, and not feel vulnerable out in the open. Caregivers can also ensure a baby's safety by leaning close to the bed, floor, car seat, etc, when they pick infants up or set them down, in order to lessen the amount of empty space babies cross.

There are several ways parents and caregivers can hold their young infants. The most common hold is the cradle hold, in which adults sit or stand with the infant cradled against their chest in one arm while the other arm adds support to the legs and bottom. The other basic hold is the traditional burping hold, in which infants lie vertically against the adult's chest, with their head resting on the adult's shoulder. While one of the caregiver's hands supports the infant's head and neck, the other hand support the lower torso and bottom.

Some parents choose to swaddle their babies in the first two months to offer them even more support and a greater feeling of close comfort and nurturing. However, every baby is different, and if babies fuss or cry when being confined, they are not good candidates for swaddling. As well, after the first few months of life, babies should not be swaddled so that they can practice using their arms and legs to develop strength and control.

To swaddle, lay out a lightweight blanket on a smooth surface and place the infant diagonally in the top corner of the blanket, keeping their head free from the blanket so they can breathe and move their head. Next, bring the baby's right arm close to her body, wrap the right corner of the blanket around her, and tuck it under her. Second, fold the bottom corner of the blanket up to cover the infant's legs. Then bring the infant's left arm close to her body and fold the left corner of the blanket over the left arm and the other folds in the blanket, finally tucking it under the baby.

As babies get older and are better able to support their own head and neck and sit up on their own more, caregivers can use the hip straddle hold. In the hip straddle, position the baby by straddling his legs over the adult's hip, using that arm to support the baby's weight sitting up. This carry allows caregivers a spare arm and hand to do other things while holding baby.

Facilitating Growth and Movement

The first year of life is a time when babies strengthen their muscles and bones and learn how to use their bodies to move around and to manipulate their environment. If babies are constantly held and carried during the first year, they will lose valuable opportunities to gain fine-tune skills. Parents and caregivers should facilitate movement and growth by giving babies safe environments to play and to explore on their own.

Caregivers can lay young infants on a clean blanket on the floor, surround them with clean, safe toys, and allow them to reach, wiggle, kick, and roll on their own or in play with others. Infants should also be laid on their bellies often, in order to help them build arm, back, and neck muscles. As babies mature and their mobility improves, caregivers will have to do more to ensure a safe environment safe environment for exploration.

Caregivers can also facilitate growth by engaging in developmentally-appropriate activities, such as "peek-a-boo," assisted walking, reaching activities, and other healthy activities that encourage movement. During playtime in the early months, caregivers can hold toys such as stuffed animals or rattles at different locations in the baby's lines of sight and encourage them to reach toward the object. Caregivers can also "dance" with infants as they start to stand. While playing some fun music or singing a song, lightly assist them in a standing position and guide them to move their body with the music. Babies will also start combining gross and fine motor skills by practicing play such as manipulating, and later stacking, blocks while sitting up.

In the first six months of the baby's life, caregivers find there are times they want to ensure a safe play area for the baby while they complete other tasks around the house or step out of the room for a few moments. Caregivers can purchase and utilise play yards (the new term for playpens) that meet general safety standards. As long as the play yard is assembled according to manufacturer's instructions and caregivers follow safety instructions, infants can safely and happily play for short durations. However, as infants begin crawling and especially when they begin attempting to cruise and to walk, play yards will rob babies from opportunities to try out their muscles and abilities, as they won't have space to roam and to move.

At this point, caregivers may be tempted to use walkers, believing that they will keep babies safe while allowing them to roam and practice their walking skills. Pediatricians warns parents not to use them for several reasons. Because of their increased mobility, these walkers can put babies at risk for nasty falls down stairs and other hazards. Furthermore, they actually discourage the development they were designed to encourage. Babies that spend substantial time in walkers will actually develop their leg muscles before their trunk muscles (opposite their natural development), which will impede normal development and growth.

In recent years, manufacturers have also introduced stationary walkers that don't allow babies to move from one location while still practicing walking motions. However, these also can be detrimental because they also cause the same backward muscle development and may frustrate babies as they try to use their new walking skills to move around their space.

The best option is to allow babies to safely explore and practice their cruising and walking skills while allowing parents and caregivers to supervise while doing other tasks is creating a larger-scale play yard. Caregivers can pick a space in their home or office that is convenient to other locations in the house, for example, a downstairs den that's near the kitchen and laundry room. Multiple such spaces, for example one on each level, allow easier supervision. To partition this space from other living spaces, use baby gates or other baby-safe enclosure devices to block access to dangerous places such as kitchens, stairs, fireplaces, expensive collectibles, etc.

Remove any dangerous objects from that area, such as window blind cords; sharp-edged glass coffee tables, and small objects that can cause choking. Leave things like couches, soft chairs, and coffee tables with surfaces that allow baby to hold on and use to cruise. Caregivers can purchase or create their own corner pads and other child safety tools.. Once again, with a little time, effort, and common sense, parents can create a safe and fun place where infants can learn and practice their motor skills.

Feeding and Nutrition

Just like older children and adults, infants need food and water to survive, to grow, and to thrive. Their bodies use the same nutritional building blocks that adult bodies use. During the first two years, they need to receive this nutrition in ways their developing digestive systems can handle, either through breast milk or baby formula in the first months and through prepared baby foods after age six months.

What to Feed?

For about the first five or six months of life, babies get all their nutrients from the milk they drink. New parents have a few options about how to feed their infants. They can choose to breast feed, to pump breast milk to feed by bottle, or to bottle-feed using specialised baby formula. Infants do not need any other food or water outside those three sources.

Most medical experts recommend that feeding breast milk is best because it contains the perfect combination of nutrients that build a baby's immune system unlike anything else. The mother's first milk, known as colostrum, is loaded with white blood cells and infection-fighting proteins. As well, breastfeeding allows immediate flesh-to-flesh contact, which encourages bonding even more. Research has shown many health benefits to babies as a result of breastfeeding such as better vision, fewer ear infections, better teeth alignment, improved digestion, leaner bodies, less diabetes, and more secure independence and mood. Research has also shown many health benefits for mothers too, such as less depression, less osteoporosis, less breast, uterine, and ovarian cancer, and faster postpartum weight loss.

If mothers have certain infections, such as HIV, or need to take certain medications, they may not be able to provide their infants with safe breast milk. As well, sometimes a baby's own medical condition requires them to use specialised formulas. It's important that mothers consult with their babies' pediatricians and their own doctors. Furthermore, some mothers find they need or want to return to work before their babies turn to solid foods. This can make breastfeeding difficult to schedule, and is often when mothers choose to pump and to store their milk to allow other caregivers to feed their babies.

Different families choose how to feed their baby for a wide range of medical, personal, and practical reasons, and it should be an educated decision a new family makes along with their doctor's input and supervision. Many families may use a combination of all three feeding methods before their children begin eating solid foods, so it's important to understand how each works and can be used.

When parents choose to bottle-feed, they first need to choose what kind of formula they want to give their infants. This decision should be made with close advice and supervision by a baby's pediatrician. Because of the Infant Formula Act, the Food and Drug Administration regulates all infant formula production. All infant formula meets the nutritional standards babies need. However, caregivers can choose what brand and form they want to buy. Formula can come in powder that needs to be mixed with water; liquid concentrate that needs to be mixed with water; or fully prepared formula. Parents and caregivers should select the formula form that is best suited to the needs of their baby and the family lifestyle.

As well, formula can be made with cow's milk or soy milk. Both are healthy for babies, but some parents choose the soy formula if their babies cannot digest the lactose in cow's milk or do not react well to formula made with cow's milk. Often, the final decision about what formula to use will come from experimentation until a formula is found that babies react best to and work best with the family's lifestyle. Moreover, any formulas enhanced with DHA (docosahexaenoic acid), and ARA (arachidonic acid), are especially beneficial for babies because these are fats found naturally in breast milk and help promote brain development.

How Much to Feed?

When babies are first born they eat often and at sometimes unpredictable times, and they eat varying amounts at each feeding. As they grow over the first months, their eating schedules regulate more, and they eat more at each sitting, during fewer sittings a day. It's important for new parents to consult with their pediatrician to make sure that their baby is getting the proper nutrition and growing and gaining weight appropriately. For the first three months, parents and caregivers should follow the baby's signals about when they're hungry or full. Parents don't have to force a feeding schedule on babies, but allow babies to let them know when they want more or are satisfied.

When newborns arrive, they can eat up to eight to twelve times a day at erratic times and for different durations and amounts. They may eat from just a few mouthfuls up to three ounces at each sitting. Oftentimes, breastfeeding babies will latch onto the breast even more than that or suckle even when they're not drinking just to get that comforting connection with their moms. This is a rich opportunity for mothers and babies to build that very important bond and trust. Breastfed babies may continue to eat more often than their bottle-fed peers do in the coming months. At about 4 weeks of age, babies may eat six to twelve times a day and take three to six ounces at each sitting, which can be every two to four hours. By around age 2 months, infants are eating about six to ten times a day, eating about three to eight ounces at each sitting, which can still be every two to four hours.

Around this age, as babies are sleeping for longer stretches at night, the frequency of their night-time feedings may taper. By around age 3 months, babies may be eating only six to eight times a day, eating about four to eight ounces at each sitting every two to four hours except during the night. Between the ages of 3 and 6 months, a baby's eating frequency will continue to decrease, but their consumption will continue between four to eight ounces at each sitting. Around this time, many pediatricians will suggest adding cereal to the bottles to increase caloric intake and to make the bottles more filling.

Breastfeeding

In the first few days after birth, the mother's breasts aren't making mature milk yet; they are making liquid called colostrum. This rich mixture has lots of protein, sugar, vitamins, minerals, and antibodies that infants need to start growing and thriving. Between days two and four, the mother's mature milk comes in and replaces the colostrum as the baby's food source. It may take several days for babies and new mothers to get comfortable and to create a routine with breastfeeding; however, as the team practices it often, it will become easier and more natural.

To encourage the easiest breastfeeding, mothers can do several things. They should allow their babies to nurse whenever they want to and as often as possible. The baby's suckling, along with the mother's hormonal changes, allow milk to be produced. As well, the more babies suckle, the more likely they will be able to keep the breast milk drained, preventing breast engorgement. When a mother's breasts become engorged, they can become hard and painful from being overly full of milk. This condition actually makes it more difficult physically for babies to latch onto the breast and extract the milk. As well, mothers should encourage babies to latch on appropriately so that their nipples do not become sore or cracked.

While mothers are breastfeeding, what they eat and drink is what they then in turn feed to their babies. Not only nutrients, but also medicines, illegal drugs, and diseases, including HIV, can pass from mother to child through breast milk. It's important that breastfeeding mothers remain in close communication with their own doctors and their babies' pediatricians to monitor everyone's health. While breastfeeding, mothers need to continue to take care of their bodies just as they did during their pregnancy. Breastfeeding mothers should make sure their diet is balanced, full of nutritionally dense foods, and includes plenty of water. If mothers become sick or are used to taking certain medications regularly to maintain their health, they should discuss this carefully with their doctors. Some medications are safe for babies to ingest, but others can cause extreme problems. As well, nursing mothers should continue to abstain from using tobacco products, alcohol, and other recreational drugs to ensure safe milk for their babies.

How Milk Adjusts for Your Baby's Needs?

At birth: Your first milk is colostrum, a thick, yellowish pre-milk that's high in the fats and proteins your newborn needs and easy for her to digest. It's also extremely rich in the substances that protect her against infections.

Two to five days after birth: Your milk will begin to "come in" now. This transitional milk is thinner than colostrum but far more plentiful, and higher in lactose and fat, which help your baby's brain develop. Your breasts will feel their largest and firmest now. You'll begin to feel your milk "let down," or move through your breasts—often described as a pins-and-needles sensation.

Two weeks after birth: Your milk will become even thinner and more watery, but it's still rich in nutrients. Your breasts will probably feel smaller and softer now. Mature milk becomes fattier over the course of a feeding (the first part is mainly water), so allow your baby to drink for about ten minutes before you switch to the other breast.

When and How often should you Feed?

Day 1: Your first breastfeeding session should take place within an hour of your baby's birth, if possible. This timing takes best advantage of his instinct to suckle, kick-starts your milk, and is a great way to bond. It also helps your uterus contract, which reduces bleeding. Don't worry about getting the technique exactly right at this first feeding.

After that, make sure he's latching on correctly as early as possible. If he's not, he'll be hungry, your nipples will hurt (a lot), and both of you will get frustrated—and you may decide to throw in the towel. Signs that you're both doing it right:

1. His mouth is open wide, with his lips curled out.
2. His mouth covers the entire areola, not just the nipple.
3. He's swallowing regularly and seems content.
4. It doesn't hurt you (except maybe for the first few suckles).

5. If he doesn't seem to be latching on properly, ask to see the hospital's lactation consultant.

The first few weeks: Your baby may eat as often as once an hour. Some signs your baby is hungry: smacking his lips, suckling motions, moving his head around in search of your breast, kicking and squirming, and looking alert.

From around 1 month: Once a routine is established, most newborns feed every two to three hours during the day, and around every four hours at night. Your baby should have between 8 and 12 feedings a day—even if you have to wake him up.

Almost all moms worry that their babies aren't eating enough. But your baby's appetite will ebb and flow depending on his needs; the quantity of your milk will adjust in kind. He'll be hungrier during growth spurts, which often occur at 3 weeks, 6 weeks, 3 months, and 6 months.

From 6 months on: Once he starts solids at around this age, he'll need less breast milk. But as long as you choose to breastfeed—even if it's in combination with food and/ or formula—your milk will provide your baby with important nutrients and protection against illness.

How to Make Breastfeeding Easier?

Nursing can be physically draining. So rest as often as you can, and drink lots of water. Consider letting your baby sleep in your bedroom in a crib, bassinet, or co-sleeping attachment (a low crib right next to your bed) so you don't have to go far to feed her. Initially, nursing can be painful. A topical moisturising cream for your nipples may help—just ask your doctor which kinds are safe for your baby. And, of course, support from your partner, family, or friends can make the process easier.

Mastitis

If you have a sore breast and a fever while breastfeeding, you may have an infection called mastitis. Flulike symptoms are typical—fever, chills, headache, body aches, and fatigue—along with an area of the breast that's tender, red, and firm. Mastitis is often preceded by engorgement, an infected cracked nipple, or simply exhaustion. Ibuprofen can help reduce inflammation and pain, and ice or warm packs can also provide comfort. But you'll want to call your doctor immediately. He may prescribe an antibiotic or another treatment.

How to Increase Milk Supply?

The key to stimulating production is to empty the breasts. So if your newborn doesn't nurse vigorously, expressing with a breast pump for about ten minutes immediately after each feeding can drain most of the remaining milk. It can also help relieve engorgement and coax flat or inverted nipples to protrude more.

Breastfeeding is a wonderful way to start your lifelong bond with your child, and it has benefits for both of you. Keep in mind, though, that the choice of whether to nurse or use formula is totally up to you. If you do decide to breastfeed, be patient and get help if you think your baby isn't latching on properly. As you and your baby get used to the process, you'll get into a rhythm that's right for both of you.

Expressing and Storing Breast Milk

Mothers can make expressing milk a positive and easy experience through several techniques. The more relaxed mothers are while pumping, the easier it will be for them to express milk. As well, mothers are often better able to express milk when they are thinking about their baby or imagining their baby suckling. These thoughts trigger bonding emotions within mothers that trigger milk production and release. As well, mothers can massage their breasts before and during pumping to increase relaxation and their ability to express milk.

Mothers can store the milk in plastic bottles or in special freezer bags. Fresh milk can be stored in a clean container unrefrigerated for six to ten hours, but it should be refrigerated or frozen as soon as possible. Milk can be refrigerated for up to eight days and frozen for up to three to four months. Frozen milk can be thawed; chilled milk can be warmed by placing its container in a bowl of warm water to warm it up gradually. As it warms, swirl the milk to make sure any separated milk is thoroughly mixed again. Milk should not be warmed to hotter than body temperature, as this may break down needed enzymes and antibodies. Extra thawed milk can be refrigerated and used within the same day, but milk should not be re-frozen after it has thawed.

Selecting and Preparing Bottles

When parents choose to bottle-feed their infants either pumped breast milk or formula, they need to know how to select and prepare the bottles. There is a wide range of baby bottles and nipples on the market. Most bottles today are plastic, making them virtually unbreakable. Some bottles are angled or have special vents in the bottom to prevent babies from taking in too much air with their milk, to reduce discomfort with taking in air. Other bottles use plastic liners that decompress while babies drink, to reduce air intake. Bottles come in two sizes, 4-ounce and 8-ounce. In the first month or two, parents may want to use primarily the 4-ounce bottle because babies will rarely take more than that in a sitting; later, parents may want to switch to using the larger 8-ounce bottles.

As well, parents and caregivers can experiment with the types of nipples available and determine which style is best for their baby. It is important to remember that any nipple can come with different sized holes. Smaller holes allow milk to move more slowly out of the bottle. This is better for the youngest of infants when they are learning how to eat and how to regulate their intake. If a hole is too big in the first months and allows in too much milk, the baby can choke. Larger holes allow milk to move more quickly out of the bottle. This is best for older babies, who typically like to eat faster. If a hole is too small, it can cause frustration and gas as the baby has to exert more effort to get the milk they want.

When preparing bottles, make sure that all equipment is sanitary: bottles, nipples, formula scoops, and hands. If possible, it's best that bottles and nipples are cleaned in the dishwasher on high heat between feedings. Next, for breastfeeding mothers who pump, fill the bottles and store as directed. For formula-feeding parents, follow the directions on the package exactly to prepare safe, easily digestible, nutritious meals for baby. Bottles can be heated by either mixing hot water with the formula or putting a prepared bottle in a mug of hot water to heat it from the inside out. It's not recommended to put bottles in the microwave to heat them. Microwaves can heat milk or formula unevenly, and these pockets of hot liquid can burn the baby. Milk only needs to be slightly warm to please babies; test milk temperature by splashing a little bit on the inner wrist. If the milk is too warm, allow it to cool before feeding.

Several bottles can be prepared at one time and refrigerated for up to 48 hours before feeding. If the baby does not finish a bottle, put it back into the refrigerator within 30 minutes and use it for the next feeding. Any bottle left out for longer than 30 minutes should be thrown away to prevent dangerous bacteria from breeding and fed to the baby. For the same reason, caregivers should not mix fresh formula with a partial bottle already in the refrigerator.

How to Feed?

Babies are born knowing for the most part how to eat by instinct, but they also need to be taught some aspects to getting their food. Babies are born with a sucking reflex that allows them to drink breast milk or formula, but new mothers often have to show them how to find or to connect to that food source before they can start sucking. Whether infants are going to eat from a breast or a bottle, similar techniques can be used to get them started.

The first step is finding a comfortable, relaxing, and safe position for mother or caregiver and baby. When both are relaxed and calm, feeding will be much easier. Feeding time can be a special time not only for providing nutrition, but also for providing nurture, love, and comfort. The act of feeding creates a bond between caregivers and baby as the baby learns to trust the caregivers for their needs and the caregivers strengthen their love toward the baby. Feeding should be done in a quiet, soothing place free from environmental stressors or distractions.

No matter what style of hold the mother or caregiver uses, the baby should feel protected and close to the their body and not dangling in space. Caregivers, especially breastfeeding mothers, should find and use at least two feeding positions so that babies don't become dependent on one and feel overwhelmed if that hold can't be used for some reason. Once the infant is in a snug and comfortable position, caregivers should present the milk source, either the breast or the bottle, to the infant. Even when a mother is breastfeeding, she still needs to support her breast with a free hand throughout the feeding so that the weight of the filled breast is resting on the baby's face.

Next, get the infant interested in taking the nipple by teasing their lips with the moistened nipple, which will make them open their mouths wide. When their mouths are open, the nipple should be place directly in the middle of their mouth and baby should take a wide grasp on the nipple. If mothers are breastfeeding, they should make sure that the infant is taking in at least one inch of the areola around all sides of the nipple. Infants actually suck on the areola and not the nipple. Suckling from the nipple directly will cause lessened or no milk flow and nipple soreness for mothers. When infants latch onto the breast or bottle, the sucking reflex takes over, and they will most often begin drinking naturally. As babies get older, they will learn how to take the bottle or breast as a habit, and caregivers may not need to provide as much assistance.

Caregivers can make sure the baby is getting the milk correctly by observing their drinking. When a baby is drinking properly, their lips will be sealed around the nipple facing outward from the mouth. If the baby's lips are tucked in around the nipple, caregivers should gently try to evert the lower lip with their index finger. If that doesn't work, they should gently disconnect the infant from the nipple and try to provide it again in order to help babies latch on correctly. If a mother is breastfeeding, she needs to carefully first break the suction between the mouth and breast gently by placing her forefinger between the lips and the skin to prevent trauma to her nipple and areola. This can be considered a mother or caregiver's first opportunity to teach or to discipline their child the healthy way to do things.

Burping and Spitting Up

During and after feeding, infants need to be burped in

order to release air bubbles that can cause discomfort and pain. It's normal for babies to take some air into their stomachs while they're drinking and breathing. The number of times a baby needs to be burped during the feeding process depends on the type and amount of milk drank and the baby's individual needs. It's ideal, especially in the first few months or if the baby has a problem with either acid reflux or spitting up, that they are burped every two to three ounces of formula. If a baby is breastfeeding, mothers often burp the baby when they switch breasts.

There are two positions caretakers can use to burp a baby. They can rest the baby on their shoulder with the baby facing away, or they can sit the baby up in their lap. It is important to remember to always support a baby's head and neck during the early months before they can do so themselves. This is another opportunity to discipline and to soothe babies, because often they do not enjoy burping, especially if it's mid-bottle, and will fuss and cry. Caregivers should continue to try to elicit a burp if the baby is squirming or appears to have stomach discomfort. If the baby appears comfortable and does not burp, they may not need to burp and can end the feeding without it. Caregivers should then gently but firmly pat or rub the baby's back in order to coax the air bubbles out and stop when they hear a healthy burp.

In either position, caregivers will want to have a burp cloth, such as a receiving blanket or cloth diaper, on their lap or over their shoulder in case babies spit up as well as burp. Often caregivers become concerned that their babies are spitting up what appears to be a lot of milk. Most of the time, spitting up is normal and infants only spit up a teaspoon or two of milk, although it can look like much more. If parents are still concerned they can consult their doctors, especially if the spit-up is coloured, bloody, projectile, seems excessive, or if the baby is failing to gain weight. Some babies do suffer from gastroesophageal reflux, or acid reflux, which is a condition that causes the stomach acid to back up into the throat. The doctor may prescribe medicine to make them more comfortable, but caregivers can also adjust their feeding technique to help as well. They can feed the baby in an upright position, keep them upright up for at least 30 minutes after the feeding, and burp after every few ounces. Normally, babies with this condition will outgrow it by the time they start eating solid foods.

Feeding Solid Foods

For the first five or six months of life, babies get all their calories, nutrients, and water from breast milk or formula; at around age six months, they can begin transitioning to solid foods. Doctors recommend that parents not begin feeding their infants solids before this age for a number of reasons. First, younger infants have not yet developed the physical coordination in their mouths and throats to manage solid foods and can easily choke on baby food. Secondly, research has shown that babies are much more likely to develop food allergies to any foods they try before age six months. Lastly, young infants still need the unique nutrient compounds only found in breast milk and baby formula at this point in their life.

Most of the time, babies will communicate they are ready to begin eating solid foods. Caregivers may notice their infant watching adults eat and wanting to be involved at dining situations. In addition, babies may begin waking up in the middle of the night hungry again, even though they had been sleeping through the night for weeks or months. As well, they may continue to cry and to act hungry after feedings, especially if they're eating 32 ounces or more of formula or breast milk in a day. However, it's important to discuss solid food introduction and options with the pediatrician to make sure that baby's unique nutritional and medical needs are being addressed.

One of the first solid foods parents can give their infant is baby rice cereal mixed with formula or breast milk. Caregivers can now give the baby both a bottle or breast and some cereal for about two meals a day. Rice cereal made especially for babies is fortified with the iron and other nutrients they need, and adding formula or breast milk increases its nutritional value. As well, babies will try the cereal more easily because they'll recognise the scent and taste of the milk. After a few weeks or a month of feeding cereal in addition to bottles or breast, caregivers can begin gradually adding new foods. Doctors recommend trying only trying one new food a week to watch for any potential food allergies.

Around age 7 months, parents and caregivers can start to introduce pureed and strained fruits and vegetables. Parents can choose to make their own baby food, but most buy already-prepared baby foods also be fortified with extra vitamins and minerals. Some good first foods are bananas, pears, applesauce, squash, carrots, and sweet potatoes. There is now a wide variety of baby foods available. Between ages 7 and 9 months, caregivers can also begin introducing strained meats and other baby entrees, such as chicken or macaroni and cheese. Consult with the pediatrician about what is appropriate for the baby's particular needs and growth.

How to Feed Solid Foods?

When babies begin to eat solid foods, it is recommended that they eat in a high chair. High chairs allow the baby to sit at the caregiver's height to make feeding easier and to allow the baby to interact with other people during a family meal or other dining experience. Safe high chairs should be sturdy and provide a harness device to keep babies sitting safely and securely. As well, keeping the baby in one place to eat also reduces messes. When parents and caregivers first try to feed solid foods, they will have to teach the baby how to take them. It's important in the first weeks to pick times when the baby isn't overly hungry or distressed so that they have the patience to try out this new skill.

Use small plastic or plastic-coated spoons to feed solid foods. Parents can get the baby interested in taking food from a spoon by playfully opening their own mouths wide so that the baby can mimic them. During this happy playtime, caregivers can use this opportunity to slide in a small spoonful of food. In addition, caregivers can put just a little dab of pureed food on the top of the baby's lips so that when they lick their lips, they'll taste the new food. After a few initial introductions, babies cognitively understand that these new tastes and textures in their mouths are food, and they will further develop their motor skills to take the solid foods. When babies first start taking solid foods, they may still have the tongue-thrusting reflex that causes them to push solid foods out of their mouth, around age 6 months. Caregivers should not scold or try to overcome that reflex, because this could cause the baby to choke and make dining time more stressful for everyone.

If your baby seems uninterested or unable to take solid foods at first, take a break for a week or two and try it again later. Babies will also give their caregivers clues about when they're finished eating during a sitting. They may strongly refuse to open their mouths or turn their head away from the spoon. Some babies are more subtle and may just lose interest in the eating part of the dining experience. If parents are concerned that their infant didn't eat enough in one sitting, they can be prepared to offer baby food again in a few hours if the baby shows signs of hunger.

As babies grow and continue to develop gross and fine motor skills and cognitive abilities, they also mature in their eating habits and abilities. By the time babies reach 7 to 9 months of age, they can begin eating finger foods that they are able to pick up with their thumb and forefinger. At this point, they may also begin drinking water or juice from a cup if it is offered to them. They will continue to eat pureed and mashed foods and to take a bottle at this point; however, they may be able to hold their own bottle.

Also during this stage, babies are still exploring and learning about their environment, so they will reach for anything they can while eating and will try flinging, banging, and smearing foods to learn more about them. Parents and caregivers should make sure that only safe items are within the baby's reach at their high chairs, and they can minimise the mess by using large, washable bibs and high chair drop cloths to catch any spills and smears.

Between 9 and 12 months of age, babies may begin holding their own baby-safe cups and may begin using utensils, though not precisely. In the second year of life, toddlers continue to refine their eating techniques, becoming more refined at using utensils, especially spoons, on their own. As well, because more of their back teeth are emerging, they can begin chewing foods instead of just biting foods off with their front teeth.

Weaning

As babies begin to eat more solid foods, they no longer need the bottle or breast to fill their nutritional needs. However, breastfeeding and bottle-feeding do not supply only physical needs; they also fill the social, cognitive, and emotional needs of the child. Therefore, when weaning babies or toddlers, it's important not only to replace the milk with solid foods but also to replace the love and nurturing from intimate feeding times with other forms. Different medical and child development experts disagree about the appropriate time to wean babies from the breast or bottle, but the majority agrees that weaning best occurs gradually between ages 12 and 24 months. At first, caretakers could omit baby's least-favourite bottle or breast times, such as mid-morning, and replace that feeding with a special playtime or cuddling time. This way, the baby is losing a feeding but gaining a new time of love and social interaction.

During this weaning period, caregivers can choose not to offer the breast or bottle, but provide it if the child is demanding it, as not to make weaning a hostile process. As toddlers begin to become mobile around the house, parents and caregivers can enforce a rule that the child can't drink while toddling around the house. This will also decrease dependence on the bottle. This rule is good for both cups and bottles, because the constant sipping of any sugary fluids can cause tooth decay in toddlers. The most difficult feedings to wean toddlers from are often the bedtime and naptime bottles. This can be accomplished by not allowing toddlers to fall asleep with the bottle in their hands or mouths. Also, if it's time to wean and toddlers are being stubborn about letting go of that bedtime bottle, gradually water down that bottle to transition even more slowly.

Urination and Faecal Elimination

Like all living creatures, babies take in nutrients and fluids, and their bodies break them down, keep what they need, and get rid of the waste products through urination and faecal elimination. After the first few weeks of life, babies should be wetting six to eight cloth diapers or three to five disposable diapers a day. This urine output should be monitored to make sure the baby is getting enough fluids. As well, during the first six weeks of life, formula-fed infants may have one to three bowel movements a day, mostly firm and tan in colour. Breast-fed infants may have more frequent bowel movements, often one after every feeding. As well, the stools of breast-fed babies can be different colours and consistencies, depending on mother's diet. After the first six weeks, babies will have fewer daily bowel movements. Each baby is unique and can have a different elimination pattern and still be healthy. Caregivers should consult the baby's doctor if they have any questions or concerns. As babies grow older and become toddlers, their bodies continue to mature and their bowel and bladder capacity grow, allowing more time between diaper changes. This physical maturation is necessary to allow for potty training, which typically beings around the age of three.

How to Diaper?

Preparation is the key to smooth diaper changes for everyone involved. Prepare a safe and clean changing area. At home, use a changing table with a soft and easily cleaned pad on top, or use a towel or blanket spread out on a clean spot on the floor. To be prepared away from home, carry a changing pad that can be spread on the changing tables in most public restrooms or on the floor or bed at a friend or relative's house. Having these pads assures parents and caregivers of a clean and comfortable place to change their baby wherever they go. Before the actual diaper change, have clean diapers, wipes, diaper rash cream, a spare towel, and a special toy within easy reach.

Caregivers can choose which type of diapers they want to use on their babies, cloth or disposable. Each has its benefits and drawbacks. Cloth diapers are cheaper, but their use creates more laundry, is less convenient away from home, and requires the use of sharp pins. They are also more prone to leaking. Disposable diapers are much more convenient and come in a large array of styles, but they are more expensive over time and create non-biodegradable waste in landfills. Parents should choose diapers depending on their lifestyle, preferences, and the needs of their child.

Babies may squirm and resist diaper changes, especially as they get older and stronger, because they do not like to be restrained or they just like to move and explore. Keep babies still and interested by reserving a special toy, song, or game only for changing times. The more caregivers can engage their babies mentally and emotionally during this time, the smoother the change will be. This is another prime opportunity for caregivers to bond and to build trusting relationships. No matter what parents do to keep their babies calm and still during changing time, they should always have at least one hand on them at all times to prevent any falls or injuries. If a baby or toddler is extremely squirmy, change diapers primarily on the floor to prevent falls from the changing table.

Begin the diaper change with good hand washing. To change a baby's diaper, remove the bottom half of the infant's clothing. Baby "onesies" that snap between the legs make diaper changes especially easy. Then remove the old diaper and quickly examine the contents in order to monitor the baby's health and digestion. Next, gently wipe the bottom clean with baby wipes to remove any urine or faecal matter. Be careful to wipe from the urethra toward the anus (front to back) and never in the opposite direction, to prevent germs from faecal matter infecting the urethra or vagina. Baby wipe warmers can make wipes feel better than cold wipes for cleaning. Some babies have sensitive skin that may react to baby wipes, so caregivers can also use a washcloth dampened with warm water.

Allowing babies to dry a few seconds before putting a diaper back on can help discourage diaper rash. Baby powder is no longer advised because inhaling the powder can be damaging for babies. During this period of the time when babies are diaper-free, caregivers should be prepared to be sprayed, because babies often like to urinate while naked and free. A towel over the shoulder can be the best defence for this type of incident. If babies are suffering from or often suffer from diaper rash, liberally apply a diaper rash cream containing zinc oxide to the infected area to help discourage wetness and irritation and to help the healing process. Then stretch out a clean diaper under the baby and fasten it in place. Dispose of wet or soiled diapers, and be sure to wash your hands or use a liquid hand sanitiser before resuming other activities.

Bathing

In order to stay clean and healthy, babies need to be bathed regularly. There are different ways to wash babies, according to their age, motor abilities, and preferences. Some caregivers may want to bathe their babies daily; however, to prevent dry skin, most babies receive a bath every other day or when they have an especially messy diaper. As well, they may not need to have their hair washed more than once a week, especially if they have dry, flaky skin patches on their head, a condition known as cradle cap. Bath time can be a fun and special time between infant and caregiver that can add to their physical, mental, and emotional growth. No matter how old the baby is, parents can sing and talk to their infants to increase bonding and trust. As babies grow older, they can begin to explore and learn about their body parts during tub time and can begin to play games in the tub.

The first baths newborns will receive are sponge baths, which do not require full body immersion into water. Just as in diapering, good preparation before the bath ensures a more successful bath time. Collect some lukewarm water, baby shampoo, body wash or soap, soft washcloth, warm towels, and a fresh diaper. To sponge bathe baby, first undress the baby down to their diaper, bundle them up in a towel to keep them warm, and then lay them on a firm and padded surface like a counter top or changing table. As well, just as in diapering, always have one hand on the baby to prevent falls.

Gradually clean and dry the baby part by part, from head to toe. First, gently wipe and blot the face with a warm, damp, slightly soapy washcloth, then rinse in the same manner with a soap-free washcloth and gently pat dry with a towel. Next, wash the head and hair the same way, or carefully try to run lukewarm water over the baby's head into the sink, to wash and rinse the hair. Then wash the rest of the body in the same manner, going from neck to chest, to arms, stomach (being careful to avoid the umbilical cord stump), legs and feet. Next, babies should be carefully flipped onto their stomachs on the surface so caregivers can wash and dry their back. Rotate the baby back over onto their back. After removing the diaper, gently wash and dry the genitals and finally the bottom, washing from front to back. To prevent infection, do not immerse the baby in water until the cord site is healed. Caregivers with sons should be prepared with an extra towel in case the boys choose to spray, which they often like to do when naked. When baby is clean and dry, caregivers diaper and dress baby warmly.

As babies grow and after their umbilical stump falls off, they can take submersion baths in the sink or bathtub. There are many different chairs and bathing seats caregivers can use to help keep babies steadier and safer in the tub. Some bathing seats allow babies to lie somewhat propped up to receive their bath in the sink or tub. As babies grow older and are able to sit up on their own, they can sit in a seat that looks much like a walker inside the bathtub. Babies can also take baths with caregivers, and this option is often useful for babies who do not like the water or do not like to feel alone in the water.

No matter what safety seat or method caregivers use, a baby should never be left alone in any depth of water. Babies can easily fall over and drown in water less than an inch deep. Parents or caregivers should stay with the baby at all times during bath time. Bathing in the tub is much like the sponge bath, as caregivers can wash and rinse baby from head to toe, part by part. After the bath, wrap the baby warmly in a towel and dry the baby before diapering and dressing. If they have patches of dry skin, use baby lotion in those areas to soothe and heal the dry skin.

Baby Hygiene

Besides normal bathing and diapering, other infant care includes trimming nails and brushing teeth and gums. A baby's fingernails and toenails grow quickly and need constant care. Trim the baby's fingernails up to twice a week and toenails up to twice a month. To prevent cutting or hurting the skin, only trim the baby's nails when they are sound asleep. Because the nails are so delicate, only use rounded nail scissors to trim each nail in one motion, being careful not to trim too close to the finger itself. Never trim a baby's nails by biting them off. This method puts the baby at a much higher risk of infection.

Good dental hygiene starts even before a baby's first teeth grow in. Wipe down the infant's gums with a gauze-wrapped finger after feedings to remove any food residue and to prevent plaque build-up. This method can be continued to be used as the first few teeth come in. However, when the baby's mouth begins to fill up with teeth, use a baby or toddler-sized toothbrush and a half pea sized bit of toothpaste to clean the teeth and tongue. Parents and caregivers can get toddlers interested in tooth brushing by modelling the positive habit in front of them and use this time as a special bonding time as well. Help toddlers not to be afraid of the dentist by talking them for a visit sometime between their first tooth and their third birthday, when they can go in for a fun, painless checkup.

Dressing Baby

When selecting clothes for infants and toddlers, remember three important factors: safety, comfort, and convenience. Babies will be happiest when they're comfortable and are able to move around their environment. Parents and caregivers will be happiest when they know their baby is safe and they can easily dress, diaper, and care for the baby. Safe clothes do not have any buttons or other adornments that could rip off and create a choking hazard, or any drawstrings that could be pulled to create a tripping or strangling hazard. Comfortable baby clothes are made from cotton, because synthetic materials may cause baby skin irritation. They also have flat seams inside and out to prevent skin irritation. Often, caregivers like to dress babies up in bow ties and lace for special occasions such as holidays, weddings, and picture days; however, for day-to-day dressing, simpler outfits mean happier and more comfortable babies.

Simple clothing with easy-access features such as snaps in between the legs and around the neck allow for easier dressing and diapering. Onesie undershirts and one-piece rompers are perfect for the early months. Remember temperature when considering the baby's comfort; parents often overdress and overheat their babies. Caregivers should decide how warmly they will dress themselves and then add one light layer for the baby. It's best to dress babies in multiple layers that can be added or removed according to temperature. Warm socks with elastic ankle bands and little caps are also good for keeping babies warm and snug. While shoes may look cute, babies do not really need them until they're beginning to walk and are walking outside.

Parents should have enough clothes so they won't have to do laundry every day and so they have extra clothing in case of extremely messy diapers or excessive spitting up. However, they also do not want to buy too many clothes because babies outgrow clothes faster than they wear them out. A basic baby wardrobe, or layette, could contain three to five receiving blankets, five burp cloths or cloth diapers, two to three hooded towels, six pairs of socks, five bibs, five sleep sacks or sleepers, five one-piece tee-shirts that snap at the crotch (onesies), five one-piece outfits or rompers, five outfits of separate tops and bottoms, one to two larger shirts or sweaters for layering, two soft hats, and any appropriate seasonal wear such as a snow suit or jacket. As babies begin to grow into toddlers, their wardrobe will grow along with them. When they begin walking, parents may want to purchase a pair of sturdy, comfortable, slip-resistant shoes.

Baby Sleep

Ask a mom of a newborn about her child's sleep and she'll likely look at you through bleary eyes and mutter,

"What sleep?" The fact is, it's perfectly normal for babies to have erratic sleep patterns—some rest for little more than an hour at a time! But all of them need as much sleep as they can get in order to develop properly.

Setting a sleep schedule, especially once your child is at least 6 months old, is a good way to make sure she's getting enough rest. Make naptimes and bedtimes as consistent as possible, and build in a cushion of time beforehand to help her unwind—show her a book, rock her, or give her a warm bath before bed.

How Much Sleep do Babies Need?

The number of hours of rest a baby needs varies with age. Here's what doctors recommend:

Age: 1 week *Day sleep*: 8 hours *Night sleep*: 8 1/2 hours *Total*: 16 1/2 hours	***Age: 1 month*** *Day sleep*: 7 hours *Night sleep*: 8 1/2 hours *Total*: 15 1/2 hours
Age: 3 months *Day sleep*: 5 hours *Night sleep*: 10 hours *Total*: 15 hours	***Age: 6 months*** *Day sleep*: 3 1/4 hours *Night sleep*: 11 hours *Total*: 14 1/4 hours
Age: 9 months *Day sleep*: 3 hours *Night sleep*: 11 hours *Total*: 14 hours	***Age: 12 months*** *Day sleep*: 2 1/4 hours *Night sleep*: 11 1/2 hours *Total*: 13 3/4 hours

Sleep Soothers

Can't get your baby to sleep through the night? Try these:

Swaddle

Being wrapped tightly helps newborns feel secure. To swaddle your baby:

1. Fold down one corner of a square receiving blanket—lightweight cotton flannel works best—and place your baby in the middle, her head above the fold.
2. Pull the left side of the blanket snugly across her body, making sure her right arm is across her chest or by her side.
3. Bring the bottom of the blanket up over her feet, tucking the tip under the fold right below her neck.
4. Place her free arm against her side; fold the other end of the blanket over her body.

Massage

Babies and toddlers who are massaged for 15 minutes before bedtime fall asleep sooner and are more likely to sleep through the night than those who are rocked to sleep.

Let Baby Suck her Thumb

It is her way of soothing herself—which is key to helping her learn to fall asleep on her own—and studies show it may be protective against SIDS.

Provide Loveys

Transitional objects like a teddy bear or blankie help make bedtime less lonely for babies. If your baby rolls over regularly (usually at around 5 months old), she's capable of moving away from a suffocation hazard, so there's less risk of SIDS. A small, crib-size blanket is also fine for a baby 6 months and older, who can push it off or crawl from under it.

Get-to-sleep Strategies

The best sleep arrangement for your baby depends on many factors. Here's how to find the right baby sleep routine for your family:

Independent-baby Approach

Establish a bedtime routine—including a bath or massage, for example—that lets your baby know bedtime is near. After soothing him, put him down while he's drowsy but still awake, to help him learn to fall asleep on his own. By 6 weeks of age, a longer sleep period (about four hours) will emerge at night. Both you and your baby are take-charge types who prefer order and predictability—for instance, if he immediately knew how to latch on and smiled at exactly 6 weeks. With these "easy" babies, bedtime may be effortless compared to what other moms go through.

He'll-get-it-when-he's-ready Approach

This is the polar opposite of the independent-baby approach. If your baby prefers rocking, you rock. If he prefers sucking, you nurse or rely on a stash of pacifiers. Not many sleep experts will endorse this laissez-faire approach to bedtime. Yet many parents follow it. You're a very patient person. You see no need to nudge your baby into a routine before he's ready.

All-together-now Approach

A co-sleeper or bassinet next to your bed is safest, but many parents sleep with their baby right in their own bed. Co-sleeping can work as long as you remember that the baby's bedtime is before yours and that you'll have less room and will have to be careful not to roll over on him. Also, to keep him safe from SIDS, you'll need to put him down on his back; keep him away from comforters and pillows; make sure he doesn't get wedged against the wall; avoid water beds; maintain a smoke-free environment; and never use alcohol, drugs, or any medication that might make you unaware of your baby's presence and more likely to roll over on him. Parenting for you is like one great big bear hug, with lots of holding, rocking, and breastfeeding. Most babies would love this close connection, except perhaps a very active child, who might feel penned in.

Long-goodbye Approach

You're going to very slowly decondition your baby from using you as a sleep crutch. Begin by putting him to bed in his crib, while you sit on a chair next to him. If he fusses, pat his back or head to soothe him, but don't pick him up. Leave the room after he's asleep; repeat if he wakes during the night. Do this for the next three days during naps and bedtime. Then move your chair about halfway across the room and soothe him verbally only. Every three days, move farther away until you're in the hall. Typically by day 14, he's fine on his own. You can't bear the thought of hearing your baby cry for hours on end, but you want him to learn how to fall asleep on his own—soon. You may also have found that your baby's temperament isn't the easiest: He may be shy and clingy, sensitive and easily overstimulated, or high-energy and intense.

Get-with-the-programme Approach

This strategy—known as "Ferberising" because it was popularised by Richard Ferber, M.D., in his book *Solve Your Child's Sleep Problems*—is best used after 4 months (you should always respond quickly to newborns) and before 8 months so your baby hasn't fallen into hard-to-break habits. Begin by putting him down when he's drowsy but still awake. If he cries, console him by talking softly and rubbing his back. Leave the room for a brief period—about five minutes at first—then return to console him if he's still upset. Don't take him out of the crib, though. Repeat this pattern until your baby falls asleep, and again if he wakes during the night. Each consecutive night, lengthen the time you let him fuss by a few more minutes, until it's no longer necessary—which, depending on your baby's temperament, may be a few days or a few weeks. You don't mind hearing your baby cry because you know it'll get him into a good sleep routine in the long run. Plus, your baby's not the type to get more and more worked up the longer he cries.

Baby Sleep Safety Precautions

- Put your baby to sleep on his back, even if he was born premature.
- Use a crib or bassinet in your bedroom or a co-sleeper that attaches to the side of your bed until your baby is 6 months old. He's safer there than in his own bedroom.
- Avoid having your baby sleep in your bed. Babies under 8 months old who slept in adult beds rather than cribs are 40 times more likely to suffocate or become entrapped between the wall and the mattress.
- Steer clear of loose bedding, pillows, or stuffed toys in the crib.
- Don't overbundle your baby, overheat the room where he sleeps, or smoke in the house. All of these have been shown to increase the risk of SIDS.
- Never let your baby sleep on a sofa.
- Be vigilant about how your child's caregiver puts your baby to sleep. More than 20 percent of babies in daycare centres are still put to sleep on their tummies.

Avoiding a Flat Head

Flat spots on the head (also called plagiocephaly) can develop when your baby continually rests in the same position. To keep this from happening:

— *Vary your baby's sleep position.* Most babies prefer to face the action in the room, so periodically change the direction in which you lay your child down in the crib. That way, she'll rest on different sides of her head.

— *Provide plenty of tummy time.* Let your child lie on her stomach when she's awake, and encourage her to look up. She may not like it at first, but a few minutes of tummy time each day is fine for a start. It strengthens her upper-body muscles so she can move her head around when she's lying down.

— *Limit time spent in infant seats.* Keeping your child in a position where her head rests the same way against any surface can cause a flat head. So don't leave her for extended periods in infant seats, swings, carriers, or strollers. Vary her position throughout the day, and give her plenty of upright "cuddle time."

If your pediatrician discovers any flattening of the head, she may recommend adjustments or exercises to strengthen your child's neck muscles. With these changes, most flattening improves within two to three months. If it doesn't, a specialist can determine whether further treatment, such as a "skull-molding" helmet, is necessary.

Nap Know-how

To help your child get his rest during the day, use the same strategies you use at night: Provide a pre-nap cue like reading a book or offering a favourite stuffed animal, always put him where he usually sleeps to nap, and try as much as possible to stick to regular naptimes.

Soothing a Crying Baby

When taking the stance that young infants signal genuine

needs by crying, then the message infants convey to their environment is unmistakable: Extensive close contact with their caregiver is a necessary prerequisite for their wellbeing. However, the outdated advice that parents should not give in to their infant's calls for closeness to prevent the child from learning that crying will get him what he wants, sufficient to make a spoiled, fussy baby, and a household tyrant whose continual demands make a slave of the mother.

Every mother has been there: Your baby is crying, you have no clue how to soothe her, and you'd give anything to have someone tell you how to stop it. As frustrating as crying is, simply understanding why babies do it can take some of the stress out of the situation. And fortunately, there are several things you can do to calm your baby—and make both of you feel better.

Babies can't tell us "I'm hungry," "I'd like to get out of this car seat," or "This itchy tag is driving me crazy!" So instead, they cry. It's their way of saying "Mummy, I need you!" What should you do if all of your baby's needs have been met (he's rested, fed, has a clean diaper) and he's still crying? Don't assume the worst.

All infants have periods of fussiness during their first few months, perhaps because they have an immature neurological system. And some babies are just more sensitive—noises, smells, even certain sensations can upset them. Most newborns cry for an average of three hours a day, peaking at around 6 weeks. The good news: By 3 months, most babies' crying will subside to about one hour a day.

When a baby cries, it triggers the release of the hormone prolactin (dubbed "the mothering hormone") in moms, which creates an urge to pick up the baby and meet her needs. You're hardwired to soothe your baby, and when that doesn't happen, it can make you feel like a failure. But your baby's fussiness is not a reflection on your parenting skills—and it's completely normal for a baby to cry even when there doesn't seem to be a direct cause. If you're ever in doubt, however, don't hesitate to call your pediatrician to make sure there isn't an underlying problem.

Simple Soothing Strategies

Not every strategy will work for every baby, and some techniques may only work at certain times, depending on your baby's mood. The key is to experiment; over time, you'll figure out what's best for your baby, and when.

1. *Re-create the womb.* Your infant may be fussy because he misses his first "home," so simulating the amniotic environment can calm him. Try these techniques, together or separately:
   - *(a)* Swaddle him snugly in a blanket with his arms down.
   - *(b)* Hold him while he's on his side or stomach rather than his back.
   - *(c)* Make shushing sounds, or create other white noise by running a hair dryer or fan (the inside of the womb sounds like a constant pulsing whoosh).
   - *(d)* Jiggle him gently.
   - *(e)* Give him something to suck on—either a pacifier or a finger.
2. *Use your hands.* Touch stimulates receptors in the brain that calm your baby, and research shows that long, smooth strokes tend to work better than short, brisk ones. Try caressing your infant's cheek, back, legs, or stomach. Or keep your baby close by wearing her in a front carrier. You don't have to

spend all day toting her around, but the more you touch her (giving her a mini-massage during a diaper change, for instance), the happier she'll be.

3. *Talk.* The familiar tone of Mom's voice is one of the most effective soothers for babies, according to research. So keep the chatter going—but speak quietly so your baby isn't overwhelmed.
4. *Release your inner pop star.* Singing can also be calming. To your baby, you're the ultimate star. Sing calm, slow songs, such as lullabies—the body responds to music by adapting heart and respiratory rates to the tempo.
5. *Take a drive.* Driving around the block combines steady motion and white noise. If driving isn't convenient, try a vibrating bouncy seat or swing, which also have the white-noise/movement combo.
6. *Get wet.* Many moms swear by baths to calm their babies. The sound of the running water and the warmth on the skin can do wonders for a crying baby. You can get into the tub, too, to add soothing skin-to-skin contact.
7. *Distract him.* Introduce a new toy or shift his attention to the family pet or a mirror. He may well forget all about his cranky mood.
8. *Keep your cool.* If you get frustrated, your infant will pick up on that tension and react, and this pattern can become a cycle that's hard to break. Trying too hard to calm your baby can also backfire—some simply don't like to be handled as much as others. While you shouldn't let infants under 3 months cry it out, it's okay to let them fuss for five minutes. This will give yours the opportunity to start to figure out how to soothe himself (and it may give you a chance to regroup, too).

9. *Keep doing what works.* When you find a strategy that soothes your baby, stick to it. Trying something different every five minutes can be overstimulating. Limit yourself to two or three methods that seem to work—if one fails in one instance, try the other, instead of introducing several new techniques. You almost always get results after a day or two if you stick to a consistent pattern.

Best Baby Holds

Carrying your baby helps her feel safe and comforted. A few tried-and-true methods:

1. *The cradle-carry*: With both elbows bent about 45 degrees, rest your baby's head in the crook of one arm, supporting her with both of your forearms along the length of her back. Rock or bounce her gently while patting her bottom. She may find this position especially soothing, since she can see your face.

2. *The sit-and-rock cradle*: This a great way to let your baby see her world and distract her when she's fussy. While standing, hold her against your chest, facing away from you. Place one hand under her bottom to create a "seat" and wrap the other arm around her chest for support. Sway from side to side or walk around to find a view she likes.

3. *The football hold*: Because this method puts pressure on your baby's tummy, it can help relieve gassiness. Place your baby facedown along one forearm, using the crook of your arm to support her neck. Place your other arm between her legs to support her lower body. Once you get the hang of it, you can even use one hand to prepare a bottle.

4. *The over-the-shoulder hold:* Like the football hold, this one's good for gassiness. Hold your baby's stomach against your shoulder and let her head and neck drape over it. Support her head with your hand until she's able to control it herself.

5. *The heart-to-heart:* In this position, your baby will feel extra close to you as she gets in tune with your rhythms. Hold your baby vertically, with her head resting on your chest, near your heart. Sway from side to side.

Decoding the Wails

It's not easy to figure out what your baby's various cries mean. But keep these general guidelines in mind:

- Newborns have a very distinct, high-pitched wail—and contrary to what you may think, this often doesn't indicate pain. They simply take in short, rapid breaths and let out a short crying sound each time they exhale. Older babies begin to breathe in deeper when crying, so each cry is longer.
- When he's hungry, a baby will quietly fuss and squirm. If he isn't fed, the cry will escalate. (Unless he's a newborn, and then the big wails are likely to start right away.)
- If he's in pain—from gas, teething, or illness—your baby will probably have a piercing cry and a pained look on his face. He'll also be especially difficult to console.

Strategies to Avoid

Popping in a pacifier right away. Yes, it might quiet her, but you won't get to figure out what's really wrong.

Rushing to feed. If you stick a bottle or your breast in your baby's mouth every time she cries and before you're sure she's hungry, you could be showing her that eating is a way to comfort herself. And that can eventually lead to overeating.

Trying too many different ways of soothing at once. It takes a while for soothing techniques to work. If you quickly change positions, or swaddle and then unswaddle immediately, your baby will probably become more agitated.

Baby Massage

The warm touch of your hands can console your baby instantly. In a warm, quiet room, undress him except for his diaper and put him on a comfortable surface (a bed, couch, your lap). Use baby oil or a moisturising lotion.

Apply gentle yet firm pressure with each stroke. Be aware of your baby's cues: If he wriggles or fusses, stop and try again another time. You can do this entire sequence or just the parts your baby likes. Begin with your baby on his back:

Head

1. Using your open hands, stroke both sides of the face, from the forehead to the neck and back up again.
2. Using a circular motion, stroke over the temples and the hinge of the jaw.
3. Lightly massage behind the ears and continue the circular movements over the rest of the scalp, avoiding the soft spot on the top.

Arms

1. Wrap both hands around the baby's upper arm and stroke down from the shoulder to the wrist, using a gentle, milking motion.

2. Stroke the palms of the hand with your thumbs.
3. Gently squeeze and then pull each finger.

Chest

Starting with your hands flat on the baby's chest, stroke up toward the neck, and then downward to his sides.

Abdomen

Using a hand-over-hand motion (like a paddle wheel), stroke him moving from high to low on the abdomen.

Legs

Wrap both hands around your baby's upper thigh, and stroke down toward the ankle and back up to the hip.

Feet

1. Use a thumb-over-thumb motion to massage the entire bottom of the foot.
2. Gently squeeze and then pull each toe.
3. Make small circles all over the top of the ankle and foot.

Now turn your baby facedown:

Back

1. Stroke, in a hand-over-hand motion, from the upper back to the buttocks, with the flats of your hands contoured to the shape of his back.
2. Using your fingertips, massage the long muscles next to your baby's spine with circular motions from his head to his buttocks. (Don't rub directly over the spine.) Continue massaging down his legs to his feet.

Neck

Finish by lightly massaging your baby's neck and shoulders. Crying is a normal part of your baby's life, and after some experimentation, you and your baby will figure out how to calm her down together. And take heart: After three months, her crying jags will be less frequent and much more comprehensible, so you'll be better able to decipher what she needs.

Medical Check-ups and Immunisations

Pediatricians and family doctors see babies often in the first years of life to make sure that they are growing and developing properly and to address any concerns and needs parents might have. Doctors may have their own preferences about when they want to see babies for well-baby visits, but in general, they occur once in the first two weeks of life and then again at the ages of 2 months, 4 months, 6 months, 9 months, 12 months, 15 months, 18 months, 24 months, 30 months, and 36 months. At a normal well-baby visit, parents should expect doctors to measure and weigh the baby and to discuss the baby's feeding and elimination, sleep habits, growth, development, and general well-being. Be prepared with a list of any questions or concerns for the doctor to discuss. Parents may also want to create a medical history book for their babies in order to keep track of their growth, medical concerns or difficulties, well-baby visits, and immunisations.

Another important factor in maintaining infant health is building up their immune system, or their ability to fight off serious infections, through immunisations. Parents should talk to their child's doctor about when and how they believe is the best to administer immunisations to their baby; however, there is a general list of immunisations that all infants and toddlers receive.

Vaccines have been proven safe and effective, and severe reactions are rare. Some parents or caregivers worry about giving vaccines because they believe they contain mercury that could harm the child over time. However, since a public outcry in 2001, almost all vaccine makers have eliminated mercury from their vaccines. Another public misconception is that vaccinations cause autism. No scientific study has shown that vaccinations cause autism. It seems other unrelated factors have made autism rates increase during the same period when immunisation rates went up. While no vaccine has a 100 per cent effectiveness guarantee, vaccines are effective 80 to 95 per cent of the times. Caregivers should contact their doctor immediately if they notice their baby has a fever of 105 degrees F or above, extreme, inconsolable crying that lasts more than three hours, lethargy or inability to arouse, or convulsions, which are extremely rare.

Common Baby Medical Concerns

Teething

Around age 5 to 6 months, give or take a few weeks, primary teeth begin burrowing their way from deep inside a baby's gums. Babies will continue to sprout four teeth about every four months until all twenty primary teeth appear, around age 2-½ years. Every baby develops in their own time, but parents can always consult their pediatrician or dentist if they have any concerns. Caregivers may notice the baby has begun teething because they begin waking in the middle of the night fussing, where they had previously been sleeping through the night, or begin to drool excessively. To check for incoming teeth, gently run a clean finger along the gum line to see if there is a swollen ridge of teeth attempting to work their way through the gums.

Babies can have varying levels of discomfort during teething. The teething experience will unique as the child herself. Several symptoms of teething discomfort can become evident. Because of the excessive drool, the baby can experience a rash around their mouth from the constant wetness and irritation, and diarrhoea as the excessive drool also irritates the anus. Babies can develop a cough as extra drool slips down their trachea; they may also have a low-grade fever, around 101 degree F. Babies will also experience different levels of pain while the teeth cut through the sensitive gums. Some infants may refuse to eat, while other babies may begin gnawing on everything: their fists, crib rail, toys, etc.

Caregivers can help soothe an infant's teething discomfort by providing cold teething aids like plastic teething rings placed in the freezer, an ice cube wrapped in a washcloth, or a cold food, such as a frozen banana. Be aware of choking hazards or food sensitivities when providing babies with frozen food items. Parents and caregivers can give infant acetaminophen if the baby appears particularly uncomfortable. From the above teething symptoms, it can be difficult to differentiate teething from other conditions described through this passage. Whenever parents or caregivers question the origins of an infant's symptoms, they should contact their health care provider.

Colic

One non-infectious physical problem infants experience is colic, which is ongoing stomach discomfort. Doctors and researchers are still trying to determine what causes colic, but they do know how to recognise it and how to soothe a colicky baby. Infants most often experience colic in the first three months of life, for varying lengths of time. When infants have colic, they will have long crying spells that may last three to four hours at a time, often starting every evening around the same time. During these crying spells, they will be difficult to comfort and soothe, and may show signs of physical discomfort such as distended belly, gas, and frequently pulling their legs up to their belly.

Caregivers should try any soothing methods they know to comfort baby. One particular method to use to soothe a colicky baby is the colic hold. Caregivers should cradle the baby facedown in their arms and position the baby's belly on their cradling palm, allowing the baby's head to rest in the crook of their arm and the feet to dangle down. Caregivers can use their other hand to stabilise the hold and rub the baby's backs. They can also sit and hold the baby belly-down on their knees while rubbing their backs. Either holding position helps relieve the gastrointestinal discomfort.

Coughs and Colds

One of the most common communicable diseases babies can "catch" is the common cold. Originating from either a virus or bacteria, colds create symptoms of stuffy and runny noses, scratchy and sore throats, coughs, irritability, and perhaps fever. Most often, cold symptoms can be treated at home, but sometimes a doctor's assistance is needed. To care for babies with colds and coughs, make sure they are getting enough fluids, use either a vaporiser or humidifier to help moisturise and clear breathing passages, and use a bulb syringe to help clean out their noses, especially before feedings and sleep times.

If any nasal discharge is clear and the infant is behaving normally, they probably do not need to go to the doctor. However, if the discharge begins to thicken and turn green, or if the baby begins to become irritated by the cold's disruption of eating, sleeping, and playing, it's time to visit the doctor. Especially in young infants, a fever, sore ears, a severe, persistent cough that keeps baby awake and creates thick, yellow-green mucus, and puffy, discharging eyes also indicate a trip to the doctor. Sometimes coughs and colds can turn into more severe conditions, such as croup or ear infections.

Croup is a disease that creates upper respiratory distress and often creates coughs that sound like barking seals. With an ear infection, fluid is caught in the middle ear and harbours bacteria that create pus and mucus, which then place pressure on the eardrum, creating extreme pain and pressure. Babies who develop ear infections will often be cranky and irritable, resist lying down, have difficulty sleeping, cry significantly, vomit, and possibly have drainage from the ear if the eardrum ruptures. Today, some doctors monitor ear infections for a few days before they prescribe antibiotics, but often, antibiotics are needed to resolve the infection and reduce the pain and swelling in the ear. If caregivers are ever in doubt, they should call their pediatrician.

Fever

Fevers are not diseases themselves, but symptoms of another disease, but they can cause the most concerns in caregivers. If parents or caregivers think that the baby feels warm to the touch, they should take the baby's temperature. The most accurate way to take a baby's temperature is to do so rectally, with a glass thermometer. To make this procedure as easy as possible, position the baby stomach down on a changing table or lap to stabilise them, while carefully inserting the well-lubricated thermometer tip one half to one inch inside the baby's rectum. Hold the thermometer in place for three minutes by stabilising it between the second and third fingers while cupping the baby's buttocks. Once again, caregivers can use songs and talking to help soothe and entertain babies during this uncomfortable time. Never force a baby to have a temperature taken rectally. Another way to take a baby's temperature is to hold the thermometer under the baby's arm and add up to two degrees. Ear thermometers are not reliable in babies under the age of one year.

Babies have a fever if their temperature is above 100.4 degrees F. Report any fever in infants under the age of three months to a doctor. It's not how high a fever goes that should concern caregivers, but rather how babies react to the fever and to the treatment that should warrant concern. If babies continue to interact and play, eat, and sleep, and if they seem to respond to fever-reducing measures, monitor the fever for a few hours and wait to call the pediatrician until daytime hours. When babies have a fever, appear and act sick, and do not respond to fever-reducing treatments, there is more of a concern. If infants under three months of age are lethargic, drowsy, not eating, and generally look and act sick while having a fever, call the doctor immediately.

To treat or to monitor a fever, caregivers can do several things. They can adjust the environment to the baby's temperatures. Remove a layer or two of clothing or unbundle the baby, and make sure to give them plenty of fluids, either breast milk or formula for infants or juice, water, and clear liquids to older babies. Parents and caregivers can also give fever-reducing medication such as acetaminophen or ibuprofen, as directed by the doctor or medication label. These medications come in baby-friendly formulas such as infant drops, children's liquid, and chewable tablets. Caregivers can give the baby a soothing bath in lukewarm water that is neither too hot nor too cold. Parents should call the doctor anytime they are in doubt or feel that these methods are not easing the fever or the discomfort.

Diarrhoea and Vomiting

Diarrhoea and vomiting can have several sources including food allergies, and infections. Rarely, severe medical conditions may require surgery. It's important to monitor these conditions, to prevent dehydration, and to communicate with the pediatrician as necessary. If parents have just recently added a new food to the infant's diet or changed formula and the baby is experiencing diarrhoea, has a rash around their anus, and appears generally well, the culprit is probably a food sensitivity or allergy; adjust the baby's menu as tolerated. If the diarrhoea is frequent, green, contains mucous, and/or is explosive, and the baby appears and acts sick in other ways, it's probably an infection.

To determine if the baby is becoming dehydrated, monitor their fluid eliminations. The baby's cries should be tearful, and the baby should be wetting at least four diapers a day. Dark yellow, wet diapers can indicate dehydration, as the urea concentration is very high. If caregivers can weigh the child, a dramatic loss of 5 percent of body weight indicates dehydration. Caregivers should contact the doctor or pediatrician if they're concerned that the baby is dehydrated, appears extremely sick and lethargic, or has vomited twice in the last 24 hours.

If the baby is acting sick and is having mild diarrhoea, stop any dairy products, juices, and fatty foods. If the baby is acting sick and having severe, explosive, watery stools every two hours, or are acting sick, vomiting, and having diarrhoea, stop all solid foods, juice, and formula. Breastfeeding mothers should continue to breastfeed, because breast milk is non-irritating to young digestive systems and can even be healing. Withhold the irritating foods for 12 to 24 hours and begin oral rehydration while the digestive system heals.

Breast-fed babies can continue to breastfeed in order to get the proper balance of fluids and electrolytes needed to prevent dehydration. Babies who are not breastfeeding can drink an oral electrolyte solution, such as Pedialyte, to hydrate them and replenish necessary electrolytes. Use a product such as Pedialyte instead of beverages such as juice, ginger ale, and sugar water, because those old home remedies will only agitate digestive tracts and do not provide necessary electrolytes. After 12 to 24 hours, gradually bring formula and other solid foods back into the baby's diet. As vomiting ceases and stools become firmer, the baby can eat more solid foods. Always consult the doctor when having any question about vomiting, diarrhoea, and the transition back to regular foods.

Nurturing Infants

While good nutrition, sleep, hygiene, and basic medical care obviously are important to babies' overall health, another less concrete element is equally important, if not more important to a baby's emotional, social, and physical health. Babies need to be loved and nurtured from birth to create a trusting bond between them and the adults who care for them, and to help create trust and interest in the world at large, which enables them to grow and to learn. In fact, even if babies are given all their basic physical needs but not given love and nurturing, they can stop growing and gaining weight, become sickly, and be diagnosed with a condition known as failure to thrive.

The most valuable loving and teaching moments often come during everyday activities. Any event can be an opportunity for showing affection and loving interaction: bath time, feeding, diapering, and bedtime, just to name a few. Parents and caregivers should constantly talk to and interact with the baby. They can describe what they're doing while they do it, and describe things in the environment. They can ask the baby questions, even if the baby can't yet respond. Caregivers can also sing, laugh, read, and pray, or participate in other religious traditions, with the baby. Not only will this interaction improve social skills, it will also help develop the baby's language comprehension and expression skills. As well, caregivers can take every opportunity to hug and kiss and to tell their baby that they love them. Hugs and kisses can never spoil a child; they can only build a child's self-confidence and feelings of security and love in the family.

Loving, nurturing family and playtime can also be a scheduled part of the day. Parents and caregivers should spend a period of time each day dedicated to playing with the baby and to stimulating the baby's minds and senses. There are many age-appropriate songs, games, and interactive toys to help develop baby's gross motor skills, fine motor skills, language, cognitive skills, and social skills. Many books available at the library or bookstore include hundreds of fun songs and games that help baby grow without having to spend a lot of money on any specific toys or props.

It is important to follow baby's lead about playtime. Babies can be over stimulated or under stimulated. Babies tell caregivers that they're feeling overwhelmed or tired by averting eye contact, disengaging from play, or actually moving away. Allow babies a chance to take a break and come back to the play later.

Dedicating a portion of every day to family play time helps the entire family grow together and will set a precedent that can build and strengthen relationships that span into childhood, through the tumultuous adolescent years, and into adulthood. These family times are especially important if one or multiple caregivers are working outside the home, and the babies spend a significant portion of time in outside childcare.

Discipline

Another way to help babies begin to learn social skills, stay safe, and begin to learn values and morals is to provide appropriate discipline from birth. During the first months, the priority of discipline is keeping babies safe until they can comprehend right and wrong and the consequences of their actions. Remove problem objects or remove babies from problem areas and redirect their attention to other appropriate toys or activities to prevent safety hazards or other socially unacceptable situations. For example, if the baby grabs an expensive book off the table, gently take it out of their hands and replace it with a baby book instead. As babies grow and begin to crawl or cruise, they may wander into parts of the house or other locations where caregivers don't want them to go; just pick them up and set them back down in another area.

At this stage of development, physical punishment such as spanking is not very effective, if at all, because infants don't understand the cause and effect connection between misbehaviour and punishment. In later months, corporal punishment alone will only teach young toddlers to avoid being caught, to avoid uncomfortable punishments, and will not teach them the reasons why their behaviour was inappropriate and what they should do instead. Moreover, physical punishments can be dangerous or even deadly for young infants. Babies can suffer brain damage or die if they are shaken. If a parent or caregiver ever becomes overly frustrated with their baby's behaviour or crying, there are other options available.

By around age 6 months, babies begin to understand the word "no." Continue setting boundaries about what is right and wrong for babies to do, say, and act. Use simple and concrete directions such as "Please put that down" or "Please come back to Mommy." Caregivers set boundaries and behavioural expectations by being consistent in their rules and redirection. If parents or caregivers do not allow the baby to play in Dad's office today, they should not allow the baby to play there tomorrow; the child will become confused about what is and is not allowed. Caregivers can also use time-outs to give toddlers a chance to take a break and calm down before coming back to the action. Time-outs should last as long as a child's age, expressed in minutes. A two-year-old takes a two-minute time-out; a seven year old takes a seven-minute time-out. Consistency can be one of the most difficult aspects in discipline, but this is good practice because consistency will become even more crucial in later years when parents and caregivers want older children to follow the rules and to respect their wishes.

Parents and caregivers can help shape and mold their baby's behaviour by modelling the behaviours they want their babies to emulate. For example, if caregivers want to teach the child to brush their teeth or to eat vegetables, they should do those activities themselves and make sure they are seen doing them. Conversely, if caregivers do not want the child to do something, like use bad language, they shouldn't do it in front of them.

Young toddlers will often use temper tantrums to show their displeasure at a situation or to get their way. Toddlers, and sometimes older children, will cry and scream, stomp their feet and fists, and even lie on the floor, refusing to move. The best way to curb these tantrums is not to reward them when they do happen. For example, if a child is having a tantrum because he asked for a cookie and didn't get one, then the parent should not give him the cookie. By relenting and giving him the cookie, the parent or caregiver is telling the child that the way to get what he wants is to tantrum. The cookie would reward the tantrum behaviour. As well, excessive attention in the form of repeated phrases such as "Ishaan, stop that" or "Please, Ishaan, don't—come look at the TV" also rewards the behaviour and will encourage him to continue.

Clearly, calmly, and concisely tell the child that a tantrum is not acceptable, and then tell him what behaviour is acceptable. For example, "Ishaan, screaming and hitting the floor are not OK. Please calm down and eat your macaroni," would be all that a parent would need to say. Then ignore Ishaan's tantrum behaviours, even if they get louder or more intense, as long as Ishaan isn't hurting himself or others in the process. With the parent or caregiver remaining calm and continuing as if Ishaan's behaviour isn't bothering anyone, Ishaan will tire of putting all that energy into something that isn't going to get him what he wants. When Ishaan does come to the table calmly and eats his macaroni, praise and encourage him, "Ishaan, that was a good job calming down. Thanks for eating your macaroni. Awesome." Give him a hug and leave it at that. By praising the listening and compliant behaviours, the parent is rewarding Ishaan, and he will learn to earn rewards in positive ways.

Tantrums often occur in public, such as at the grocery store. Caregivers feel embarrassed and want to end the noise and commotion as quickly as possible. Once again, giving in or giving excess attention will only encourage a sequel to that tantrum in the future. Continue to use the same ignoring techniques with supervision to maintain the toddler's and safety

Baby Safety

Along with feeding, diapering, bathing, nurturing, and providing appropriate health care, caregivers need to provide their babies with a safe environment in which to live and to grow. Babies are naturally inquisitive and experimental as they learn to use their minds and bodies; it's important to create an environment in which babies can experiment without danger. Even in the early months before babies are mobile, there are things parents need to do in order to ensure their baby's safety.

Crib Safety

All babies need a safe place to sleep. Cribs should be evaluated before purchased or used; good cribs are labelled with the Consumer Product Safety Commission label that certifies they're safe and secure. All parts of the crib should be securely assembled, including the mattress support system. Cribs should not have a lot of extra knobs that babies can get caught on, or decorative cutouts in which their heads can get stuck. Crib slats should be no more than 2-3/8 inches apart to prevent a baby's head from being stuck. Mattresses should be firm and fit snugly in the bed to prevent pinched body parts and suffocation. Cribs should also be free of stuffed animals, pillows, and fluffy covers. Guardrails should be sturdy, and babies should not be able to unlatch them from the inside.

Caregivers should run their hands over a crib and make sure there are no splinters, tiny pinching crevices, or sharp points. If a crib is a hand-me-down, make sure that lead paint was not used in one of the earlier layers of paint; lead paint was outlawed in baby furniture in 1974. Even on new cribs, caregivers should install plastic chew guards on the rails to prevent babies from chewing the plain wood. Caregivers should also be mindful of where the crib is placed in the room so that the baby can't reach window blind cords and strangle, or get stuck between the crib and a dresser if they are able to climb out and fall. Parents should also use a baby monitor so that they can hear the baby sleeping from any room in the house.

Baby Equipment Safety

Parents use many devices to make life with babies easier and more convenient: strollers, carriers, high chairs, changing tables, and playpens to name a few. Caregivers need to make sure that these are safe for babies by seeing that they are sturdy, working in proper order, and do not have any choking, suffocating, strangling, or cutting dangers. These devices should only be used on sturdy ground and not on top of counters or other surfaces from which babies could fall. Whenever babies and toddlers are seated in strollers, carriers, or high chairs, they should always be buckled in with the provided harness to keep them in place and to prevent them from falling or sliding out. Some caregivers use straps on the changing table as well. Even if a strap is used, never leave a baby unattended on a changing table. Caregivers should also never leave a baby alone in a bathing chair or in the tub, no matter how little water is there. Finally, parents and caregivers should never use baby walkers. These hazardous devices have been responsible for many falls, cuts, burns, and other baby injuries, and they actually hinder development because they encourage babies to develop their legs before their torsos, which is opposite from natural muscle development. This can cause gross motor development problems later in life.

Car Safety

Make sure infants are always buckled in safely in an approved car seat when a car is moving. The safest place for infants to ride in a car is the middle of the back seat. Parents may prefer having babies in the front seat so that they can watch and soothe their babies, but this is a very dangerous spot for infants in case of an accident. Babies and children under the age of twelve should never ride in the front of a car with activated air bags. It's safer for parents to pull over to console a crying baby than to bring them up front while continuing to drive.

Safety on the Move

As babies become more mobile and start to develop their gross and fine motor skills, they will want to grab, climb, put into their mouth, and play with anything they can. Parents and caregivers need to childproof their homes to prevent the baby from having access to poisonous substances, items that could burn them, items they could choke on or otherwise hurt them, and objects they could trip over while walking.

5

Parenting of Toddlers

Toddler stage is an exhilarating time for both children and parents. Young ones start to gain increasing amounts of independence. They move from "toddling" to learning to ride a tricycle or bicycle with training wheels. They learn to scrub themselves in the bathtub. Better yet, they will master using the bathroom by themselves. However, these little people aren't totally self-sufficient quite yet. Young children still need plenty of adult care and guidance.

All parents of toddlers have one thing in common—they all have to renounce their "normal" lives and start living like abnormal people! Many parents would readily confess that the toddler years are some of the most trying. They will have to cope with highly-charged and inquisitive young minds, live with their frightfully demanding and beyond reasoning temperaments and deal with their huge tantrums and sometimes absolutely unreasonable demands.

Toddler Feeding and Nutrition

Babies grow at a lightning pace—3 inches or so every 3 months. A toddler, in contrast, grows at a much slower rate—only 3-5 inches in an entire year. While growth slows somewhat, nutrition remains a top priority. It's also a time for parents to shift gears, leaving bottles behind and moving into a new era where kids will eat and drink more independently. The toddler years are a time of transition, especially between 12-24 months, when they're learning to eat table food and accepting new tastes and textures. Breast milk and formula provided adequate nutrition for your child as an infant, but now it's time for toddlers to start getting what they need through a variety of foods.

How Much Food Do They Need?

Depending on their age, size, and activity level, toddlers need about 1,000-1,400 calories a day. From the diet chart to get an idea of how much your child should be eating and what kinds of foods would satisfy the requirements.

Use the chart as a guide, but trust your own judgement and a toddler's cues to tell if he or she is satisfied and getting adequate nutrition. Nutrition is all about averages so don't panic if you don't hit every mark every day—just strive to provide a wide variety of nutrients in your child's diet.

Talk with your doctor about specifics for your child. And younger toddlers may not be eating this much—at least at first. When a range of amounts is given, the higher amount applies to kids who are older, bigger, or more active and need more calories.

Milk

An important part of a toddler's diet, milk provides calcium and vitamin D to help build strong bones. Toddlers should have 500 milligrams of calcium and 400 IU (International units) vitamin D (which aids in calcium absorption) a day. The calcium requirement is easily met if your child gets the recommended two servings of dairy foods every day, but this amount provides only half of the vitamin D requirement. In general, kids ages 12 to 24 months should drink whole milk to help provide the dietary fats they need for normal growth and brain development. Reduced fat (2 per cent) milk may be given if overweight or obesity is a concern, or if there is a family history of obesity, high cholesterol, of heart disease. After age 2, most kids can switch to low-fat (1 per cent) or non-fat milk. Your doctor will help you decide which kind of milk to serve your toddler.

Some kids initially reject cow's milk because it doesn't taste like the familiar breast milk or formula. If your child is at least 12 months and having this difficulty, mix whole milk with some formula or breast milk. Gradually adjust the mixture over time so it becomes 100 per cent cow's milk. Some kids don't like milk or are unable to drink or eat dairy products. Explore other calcium sources, such as fortified cereals, calcium-fortified soy beverages, broccoli, and calcium-fortified orange juice.

Meeting Iron Requirements

Toddlers should have 7 milligrams of iron each day. After 12 months of age, they're at risk for iron deficiency because they no longer drink iron-fortified formula and may not be eating iron-fortified infant cereal or enough other iron-containing foods to make up the difference.

Cow's milk is low in iron. Drinking a lot of cow's milk also can put a child at risk of developing iron deficiency. Toddlers who drink a lot of cow's milk may be less hungry and less likely to eat iron-rich foods. Milk decreases the absorption of iron and can also irritate the lining of the intestine, causing small amounts of bleeding and the gradual loss of iron in the stool.

Iron deficiency can affect growth and may lead to learning and behavioural problems. And it can progress to anaemia (a decreased number of red blood cells in the body). Iron is needed to make red blood cells, which carry oxygen throughout the body. Without enough iron and red blood cells, the body's tissues and organs get less oxygen and don't function as well.

To help prevent iron deficiency:

- Limit your child's milk intake to about 16-24 ounces a day.
- Serve more iron-rich foods (meat, poultry, fish, enriched grains, beans, tofu).
- When serving iron-rich meals, include foods that contain vitamin C (tomatoes, broccoli, oranges, and strawberries), which improve the body's iron absorption.
- Continue serving iron-fortified cereal until your child is 18-24 months of age.

Talk to your doctor if you're concerned that your child isn't eating a balanced diet. Many toddlers are checked for iron-deficiency anemia, but never give your child a vitamin or mineral supplement without first discussing it with your doctor.

Toilet Training

Most parents want to know the earliest date they can start toilet training. Since children mature at different rates, it is impossible for us to provide a hard and fast date when it is first appropriate to start training. Each child is unique and will become ready to start the toilet training process at his or her own "right" moment. On average, most children in India start toilet training between 18 and 32 months old. Because children normally don't walk up to their parents and say, "I'd like to start potty training, please," parents need to learn the signs and signals that indicate children are ready to begin. Primarily, children show physiological, or bodily, signs that they're ready to start toilet training. These signs happen only when young children's excretory and digestive systems have matured with age; something they have no real control over. There is little or nothing parents can do to hurry children's necessary physical maturation along.

When the natural maturation process occurs, young children's bowel movements start to become more regular, occurring between 1 and 3 times each day. As well, caregivers will notice that children's diapers are often dry, or that at least two hours pass between each wet diaper. This indicates that children's bladders and sphincter muscles are growing larger and stronger, and are able to hold back urine for longer periods of time.

Somewhere around 18 months of age, toddlers start to realise that they create waste in their diapers. Later on, they will start to notice that elimination is occurring, or notice the physical sensations that means they're going to eliminate waste soon. They demonstrate this awareness by grabbing at their diaper or standing or crouching differently so as to be more comfortable as they eliminate. Though their awareness of elimination may have started, children are not yet able to control the physical process of elimination quite yet.

When children are older, they communicate their readiness for toilet training by showing a dislike for wet or soiled diapers and a clear desire to take them off. Children may come to a parent and ask to be changed, or they may just strip off their clothes and diaper in the middle of an activity.

Young children show that they are cognitively ready to begin toilet training by demonstrating several different skills. First, children need to be able to understand and use basic words such as potty, toilet, diaper, poop, pee, penis, etc., to describe elimination and related terms. This list of words are commonly used in America currently, but there is nothing special about these particular terms. Families can use different words if they have preferences. Some families are more comfortable with anatomically correct terms, while others prefer to use euphemisms for body parts. What is important is that children begin to demonstrate a command of language that can be used to describe elimination.

Young children must also be able to understand and to follow simple verbal directions or commands. For example, they should be able to walk where indicated, stay seated when asked to do so, pick something up when asked, and so on. They also need to be able to follow multiple directions given at once, including two or three-step instructions that convey sequences of events, such as "Take-off your pants and then sit down." Children also need to be able to communicate their general needs and bodily functions to adults. Children's ability to describe what is happening with their bodies allows them to signal when they feel the urge to use the toilet, and to tell adults when they're peeing or pooping. If these cognitive and language skills have not yet been mastered, children and parents may become frustrated trying to juggle all of the coordinated steps and skills described above that are necessary prerequisites for toilet use.

There are also emotional signs that children are ready to begin the toilet training process. Parents may notice that their toddlers go off to a quieter or more private place (like behind the couch) when they have to soil their diapers. This desire for privacy shows that children not only recognise that they're passing waste, but also that they recognise the act of elimination as something which is expected to be done in private. Young children will send additional emotional signals of their interest in toilet training by showing interest in their parents' toileting habits and what happens to the waste.

Another emotional skill that children may demonstrate just prior to their being ready to toilet train is the degree of patience and maturity necessary for them to sit in place while doing a quiet activity like reading. On a larger scale, children will begin to show an overall desire for independence, wanting to show off their abilities and insisting that they can do things for themselves. This emotional maturity will be necessary for children to complete their business on the toilet.

Finally, children must have developed a range of motor skills reasonably well before they can hope to be successful using the toilet. Young tots need to have developed fine motor skills sufficient to dress and undress themselves in a quick and easy manner. Children who fumble about before being able to take off their pants and other clothing items are likely to have accidents and to become rather frustrated.

Gross motor skills are also essential for toilet training. Children need to be able to mount and get off the potty seat, toilet, or step stool easily and without knocking it over or causing it to fall off (or into) the toilet. An ill-timed dunk may, understandably, keep children from wanting to try the toilet for a while.

Pre-toilet Training

It is important that parents try not to initiate actual toilet training until children are ready. This said, there are various ways parents can work with children who are not yet ready so as to provide them with a solid foundation for future toilet training.

The simplest way parents can lay a good foundation for toilet training is to talk to children about the elimination process in age-appropriate ways. Young children can learn what is in their diapers and how it got there. Older children can be taught how their bodies make and eliminate waste. For example, mother could start up a conversation while changing her 20-month-old daughter, "Jasmin, right now you go poop and pee in your diaper, but soon enough, you'll learn how to go poop and pee in the toilet just like me and Sister Sarah."

Parents should take care to label elimination processes using terms they want children to use in conversation. Common acceptable toilet words many families teach their children include "wet", "dry", "go", "potty", "toilet", "toilet paper", "wipe", "poop", "pee", "pee-pee", "fart, "have gas", "toot", and similar words). Alternative words used to describe elimination are generally either too clinical and formal (e.g., "feces", "urine"), or considered too obscene for use by children. These early conversations about elimination help children to know what words are acceptable for talking about this sensitive subject. They represent perhaps the only time in most children's lives that frank use of potty language is not only acceptable, but actually something to be encouraged.

Parents can supplement their children's early elimination education with various children's books concerning human bodily elimination processes. Such books feature fun drawings and stories to make the topic of elimination interesting for small children, and are widely available in stores and libraries. Elimination books can be featured during children's regular bedtime or other reading times in the years and months before actual toilet training begins so as to familiarise children with the topic. There are also fun children's videos available on the subject of elimination that can be added to children's regular video viewing rotation.

Parents can help their young children to make connections between internal sensations and the elimination process. Children's ability to learn such connections forms the basis of their later ability to recognise the sensations that signal their impending need to eliminate, enabling them to seek out a bathroom and use it rather than pooping or peeing in their pants. To start this teaching process, parents should look for signs that their children will be filling their diaper soon, and point them out to children while they are happening, explaining their connection to the toilet.

To take it a step further, parents can point out when children actually fill their diapers and explain that adults and older siblings do the same thing, only in the toilet rather than in a diaper. Some parents or older siblings may be comfortable enough to let a same-sex child watch them use the toilet or to see the product and the flushing process afterward. Some children may be interested in flushing the toilet for other family members. This way, they can get used to the sounds and sights of a flushing toilet, and it will be less scary when actual potty time comes. While adult modelling of any behaviour is a strong teacher, parents will have different comfort levels in letting children observe them eliminating. Older siblings should always be asked to confirm that they are comfortable with letting younger siblings watch before this behaviour is allowed to occur.

Parent should always take care to keep their elimination-oriented discussions with children positive in nature so that children do not start feeling ashamed of themselves and their bodies. While it may feel completely normal to say, "Pewwww, that's stinky!" to children while changing their diapers, that type of talk can inadvertently shame children and discourage them from wanting to make waste and to use the toilet. Parents should stay upbeat and excited at the product in the diaper or the potty, and try to smile even if they want to gag instead. This helps children understand that eliminating waste and using the toilet are normal, positive things that "big kids" and grown-ups do all the time.

Some parents may have concerns about being too positive regarding their children's waste products, based on the notion that children may not learn this important taboo if parents don't teach it to them. A positive attitude is recommended to help shield children from thoughts that their parents think they are dirty and disgusting, and to motivate them to be interested in toilet training and to want to gain control over their elimination at the earliest realistic opportunity. It is perfectly okay for parents to teach their children not to talk about elimination outside the family, if this becomes a necessary limit to set.

Preparing the Space for Toilet Training in Early Childhood

Preparation of the actual toilet training space will make the training process go much more smoothly when it becomes time to begin actual toilet training. Many parents wonder if they should deck out their bathroom in potty training gear months before starting actual training, or instead wait until immediately before toilet training begins to unveil the potty. Both approaches have their debatable advantages and disadvantages. When a potty is set out weeks or even months before toilet training begins, children will have an opportunity to grow familiar and comfortable with it. This added comfort level helps some children become more relaxed and prepared for toilet training. Parents can allow children to play with empty, sanitised stand-alone potties and/or sanitised potty inserts. However, parents should be careful how much children play with these items, because kids still need to learn that these devices are not toys.

The flip side of children's enhanced relaxation and comfort with the potty after early exposure to it is boredom. Some children will lose interest in the potty if it is put out too early, and will not have any real interest in using it when the true time arrives. Other children really benefit from advance exposure to the potty. They feel unsettled and even scared by this new contraption when it just appears out of nowhere and may not want to go anywhere near it. Parents should think about their children's personalities when deciding which approach makes more sense for the family. As is the case with nurturing along any developmental activity, if a child becomes overwhelmed or disinterested, parents should just back down for a couple weeks and then try again later, maintaining a positive attitude all the while.

Adult toilets can be large and intimidating objects for some small children. In order to get children comfortable with the size, shape, and noise of an adult-sized toilet, parents can encourage supervised experimentation with it. For example, children can throw bite-sized cereal O's into the toilet bowl and practice flushing them away. Such experiments can help children get experience operating a toilet so that they will feel less scared of it in the future.

Safety and Sanitation

The toilet or "potty" apparatus itself is the most vital piece of toilet training equipment. Fortunately, parents have an array of options to choose from with regard to selecting toilet gear. First, families can elect to use inexpensive toilet inserts, which fit comfortably and snugly on top of regular toilet seats. Such inserts allow small children to use the standard toilet using a seat made for children's smaller bodies. Inserts are easier to move from place to place than are freestanding potties. This portability helps young children feel "at home" using the toilet, even when the family is at Grandma's house or travelling. As well, because they make use of regular toilets, toilet inserts don't have to be dumped and cleaned after each use. Children will likely need a step stool in order to seat themselves on the insert. As some children may need help climbing up and down from the toilet, it is probably a good idea to maintain adult supervision of the toileting process throughout toilet training. Some children are frightened by the large and intimidating (to a small child) adult toilet, so using toilet inserts isn't a good option for everyone.

Another choice for toilet training is the freestanding potty chair. These child-sized, low-to-the-ground chairs are generally made of tough plastic, with plastic tubs that fit under the seat to collect waste. Because these chairs are small and often come in fun shapes and bright colours, they are a nice option for children who are intimidated by the adult toilet. Their kid-friendly features can make potty chairs more fun and exciting for children to use. Also, children can often use potty chairs unsupervised, fostering their greater sense of independence. Stand-alone potties can be placed in other rooms for added convenience, allowing children to reach the toilet successfully when they aren't able to "hold it" long enough to run all the way to the bathroom. As an added bonus, children can place their feet firmly on the ground while using the potty chair, which can make bowel movements much easier. Children are too small to put their feet on the ground when using an adult toilet, even when that toilet has been fitted with an insert.

There are some drawbacks to potty chairs. These chairs are more expensive than inserts, and parents need to either buy multiple chairs for multiple bathrooms (or different floors), or resort to continuously moving the potty chair from place to place as children move through the house. Children can also confuse potty chairs for toys at times, which may make the process of toileting more difficult. As well, cleaning up potty chairs can be just as unappetising as cleaning up diapers, as the collection tubs need to be dumped, cleaned, and sanitised after each use in order to maintain good hygiene. Finally, while potty chairs are a good solution for early toilet trainees, they do not fully prepare children to use adult toilets (e.g., they do not have a flushing mechanism). It may be wise to shift children from the potty chair to a toilet insert after they have mastered use of the potty chair so as to provide a better transition to adult toilet use.

Some families elect to stick with the regular adult toilet for toilet training. The adult toilet comes without added monetary costs, and children don't have to learn how to transition to a different toilet later on in their development. Families who toilet train using adult toilets will, however, have to provide children with a step stool, as they will almost always need to climb to be able to reach a standard toilet. In addition, because of a toilet's large size in comparison to young children's small bodies, using a full-size toilet without supervision is not recommended. Children may fall off the toilet completely or fall into the water head-first. Some children become easily frustrated with adult toilets due to their large size and their being relatively uncomfortable for small bodies to use. When this is the case, families may be better off with the potty chair.

No matter what toilet kids use at home, many families invest in portable travel potties if they frequently go on long car trips or are active out in the community. These potties are often collapsible or very light-weight, so they're easy to pack and to move. Some come with bowls with lids that can be closed until waste can be dumped. Others have an absorbable, disposable liner that can be discarded in the trash can after use. Because these potties can be taken virtually anywhere, they can be used in a public restroom, on a quiet street, during a visit at someone else's home, or even in a quiet corner of a store in desperate times. Parents who elect to use such portable devices should have their children practice using them several times at home before trying to use them on the road.

Whether selecting a toilet insert, a potty chair, or a travel potty, parents should look for features that indicate quality. Devices should always be sturdy and well-built. They should also be comfortable for kids to use. Toilet seats should have a built-in splash guard for little boys to help prevent messes and splatters in the face (these seats can be turned around when little girls need to use them). Lids on potty bins should fit securely so as to reduce smells and avoid spills when waste cannot be disposed of immediately.

Beyond choosing a toilet device, families also need to set up the bathroom or other potty place so that it is kid-friendly and usable. The number one rule to keep in mind in this regard is that there should always be toilet paper within easy reach of children's small arms. Even though the traditional toilet paper dispenser may be less than an arm's reach for an adult sitting on the seat, it will be a much farther grab for little arms and may cause children who are stretching out to fall off the seat if they are using an adult toilet. If self-contained or portable potties are in use, it is also important to keep toilet paper handy for use with those devices, whether they are placed in the house or used on the road.

Wet wipes can be a useful product to purchase for use in addition to, or instead of dry traditional toilet paper. Wipes are useful for wiping bottoms as well as cleaning up associated messes. Many companies manufacture flushable wet wipes that children can use when they're first learning to wipe themselves.

Books, puzzles, and other self-contained toys should be kept within a child's reach for use during toilet time. These entertainment items will help young minds stay patient during the actual elimination process and make the toileting process more fun. Restricting certain desirable toys and books solely for use at toilet time helps keep children engaged and interested in those items and thus less likely to be bored while toileting. Toilet time can be a particularly good time to encourage children to read short picture books. Providing age-appropriate reading material helps reinforce children's love of stories and learning, and helps to develop reading skills.

Even if young children are going to learn on a self-contained potty that sits low to the ground, families will still need to invest in a child-sized step stool so that children can reach the sink in order to wash themselves after using the toilet. Step stools will allow children to reach the faucet as part of the very important hand-washing lesson; and they are also useful for brushing teeth. Parents should also make sure that there is always kid-friendly soap and a clean towel within a child's reach. Some companies make special foaming soaps for kids that come in fun colored bottles. While these features may entice some stubborn children to lather up, the extra cost these items command is not generally necessary most of the time.

Toilet Training Methods

After having educated children about elimination, and receiving the proper signals from them that they are ready to transition from diapers, parents can swing into full toilet training action. Throughout this process, parents need to communicate a positive attitude to their trainees. Parents should remain calm, warm, encouraging, upbeat, and consistent with regard to the messages they communicate to their children. Parents need to rejoice with children in their successes and to provide support and encouragement in their challenges, time and time again.

Parents also need to pay attention to their children's reactions throughout the toilet training process. Children may seem exuberant about learning to use the potty on one day, and avoidant or oppositional on the next. Parents should watch for both obvious and subtle signs that children are becoming overwhelmed and back off from toilet training for a day or two when this occurs. Parents who continually push potty training on children who do not want to participate may find that children ultimately shut down and refuse to use the toilet for some time.

In the scheme of things, it is perfectly okay to lose a few days' progress towards toilet training when a child is overwhelmed, when the alternative is to lose a month or more due to regression. Toilet training tends to be a long-term project spanning months and even years, and not something that can be accomplished in a weekend. Parents who go into toilet training with the idea of providing a weekend intensive boot camp will probably do more harm than good.

One major technique used for toilet training is the practice session. In a practice session, parents take children to the bathroom and direct them through the various toileting steps during times when it is likely they will need to use the bathroom (e.g., before bedtime, after a nap, first thing in the morning, or an hour after a big meal). This strategy is also useful when young children show signs that they need to use the restroom, such as crossing their legs, doing the "potty dance," or passing gas.

During the first few practice sessions, parents may have to physically and verbally guide their children through each potty step in checklist fashion in order to ensure their success. For instance, Mummy could say, "Ok, Monu, when your bladder feels full and you feel like you have to go potty, you're going to come into the bathroom, pull down your pants and panties, and sit down on the toilet," while leading Monu by the hand into the bathroom and physically helping Monu complete these steps. Mummy can also help keep Monu entertained and patient while she goes to the bathroom.

"Letting go" of waste products does not come naturally to all young children. Some children are nervous about the process and are too tense to perform. Parents may need to encourage such children to relax and to let their bodies respond naturally. For instance, Mummy could say, "Monu, just relax. You'll feel something trying to squeeze out of your bottom. That's OK. That's your body letting go of the poop. Don't try to stop it. Just let it slide out. Take a deep breath with me. You might feel a little pee come out, too. That's OK."

Often, children find it easier to start to defecate than to urinate while sitting on the potty, so parents can instruct their children to focus on defecation first. Many children automatically urinate while they are defecating. Sometimes it may be helpful to encourage children to push a little bit in order to help themselves poop. However, parents need to watch that their children don't take this advice too the extreme. Pushing too hard or straining can make the elimination experience quite uncomfortable or painful and end up making the situation more frustrating then it has to be.

Teaching little boys to use the toilet comes with an extra layer of complication. Boys can urinate while standing or sitting, unlike girls who always sit. Often, families find it easier and less messy to start off teaching little boys to sit down while urinating and pooping because it can be difficult for little boys to keep one activity separate from the other. A little boy who sets out to pee may end up pooping too. If the little boy is standing while this happens, a mess will occur.

At some point in time, it will become necessary to teach boys how to urinate standing up. This point in time will happen faster if male role models are around and the little boys see their father or elder brother peeing while standing up. Parents just need to accept that learning how to urinate while standing up will be a messy process, and that their son's aim will improve over time.

Little boys can watch (with permission) daddy or a elder brother while they urinate standing up in order to get some pointers on how to do this properly. Parents can also make up games to help little boys improve their aim. For example, Daddy can paint a red bull's eye in the bottom of the potty chair and challenge Raju to hit the bull's eye on the centre. Or, Daddy can tear up little pieces of toilet paper and litter them on top of the water in the toilet bowl and encourage Raju to "sink" them with his urine stream. Using oat ring cereal as floating targets for little boys to aim at is another popular method. Playing games like these encourages a sense of playful competition, usually makes the potty training process more fun, and improves boys' accuracy.

"Practice makes perfect" as the saying goes. Though children require explicit prompting and physical or verbal guidance for each step of the toilet training process during their early practice sessions, after a while they will be able to produce the sequence of desired behaviours by themselves with only a single prompt by Mom that they should get started. It is best to keep an open mind during the training process. Many children will go through several first practices without actually eliminating waste. Keeping this in mind, parents should avoid forcing children to stay on the potty until they have actually gone to the bathroom. Forcing a child to remain on the toilet for an extended period can be hurtful in two ways. First, some children may view the situation as a challenge, and thereafter see how long they can avoid using the bathroom so that they can somehow "win" the "competition". Second, other children who are unsure of or even fearful about the toilet will become even more unsure or frightened if they come to view the toilet as a punishment. Either situation can lead to otherwise avoidable problems and delays.

Rather than forcing children to use the toilet, parents should offer children plenty of reinforcements (i.e., rewards) so as to encourage their toilet use whether that use results in actual elimination or not. Parents should make lots of positive encouraging verbal statements, such as "Isha, you went poop in the potty. That's awesome!!" or "Mayank, I'm so proud you sat on the potty while we read a poem together" during each step of the toilet training process. These verbal encouragements will help children to feel successful and want to repeat their successes.

Another way parents can increase children's interest in using the toilet consistently is to offer them small incentives to increase their motivation. Small but frequently offered tokens of parental pride work better for this purpose than large rewards that are not delivered until after substantial progress has been made. Many families choose to use a potty sticker chart. Parents can create a chart for the week or the month and reward the children with a sticker on the chart every time they successfully reach and use the toilet. Children can look at their stickers with pride, and use them to monitor their accomplishment. An alternative to using stickers is to reward children with one tiny bite-sized candy (or some other small valued item) each time children use the potty. Whatever incentives are offered, they will always work best when they are paired with lots of smiles, hugs, and specific verbal praise such as, "Ishaan, you remembered to go poop in the potty! That's so awesome! Good job!"

The use of small frequent incentives such as stickers on a chart can also be of great help in motivating children to perform a wide variety of desired behaviours. For example, children who forget to flush their waste or to wash their hands can be motivated to do so with a sticker chart designed to reinforce these specific habits.

Though small frequent reinforcements and incentives can be useful in motivating desirable toileting behaviours, the opposite is never true. It is never a good idea to punish children for unsuccessful potty sessions or for toilet accidents. While punishment does tend to have the short-term effect of motivating children's compliance with parental wishes, the long-term use of punishment tends to lead to children's defiant refusal to use the potty, or creates fear and avoidance of the potty. In a similar vein, parents should also be careful to not communicate disgust during the toilet training process. Subtle signs such as grimacing in response to the sight of a full potty container, and more obvious signs like saying "I hate emptying this potty," are both likely to be picked up on by children who may then become discouraged from wanting to use the potty out of feelings of shame, and embarrassment. Negative outcomes are generally avoidable so long as parents take care to stay positive and encouraging rather than punishing during the toilet training process.

Once children have figured out the general process necessary for getting themselves to the potty on time and actually peeing and pooping in the toilet device, they still will need help in completing other vital potty tasks. For example, they must learn how to wipe themselves clean. Though adults don't think twice about the cleaning process, young children find the task to be a big deal due to their fine motor skills not yet being completely developed. Parents should first verbally explain to children how to wipe themselves and why this is important. It's especially important to teach little girls how to prevent feces from getting near the vagina so that infection or irritation does not occur. Little girls should be taught to wipe from front to back when they poop, and not the other direction.

Children should practice wiping themselves each time they defecate. However, Mom or Dad should always ask for the "last wipe," so they can make sure that children's little bottoms are completely clean. Families might also want to invest in flushable wet wipes made especially for potty-trainees, as the added moisture contained in these wipes makes for easier cleaning. As young children become more independent wipers, caregivers should teach them the proper length of toilet paper to use (not too long or too short) so that they're not wasting paper or clogging the toilet with excess on the one hand, or dirtying their fingers unnecessarily on the other.

Beyond cleaning themselves, young children will need help to accomplish other important potty tasks. If kids are using a self-contained potty seat, they will need an adult to empty and to sanitise the pot each time they use that device. It is good practice for children to help flush the waste away in the adult toilet, even if they aren't yet using it. Parents will also need to supervise and direct children's hand-washing. While being sure to give kids the lead so that they feel competent, parents should take care to make sure that kids are properly washing away all dirt and germs, including in the areas under the fingernails and between the fingers that children sometimes miss.

At some point after children have figured out the general process of toileting they will be ready for the big moment when they leave their diapers behind. Once this moment occurs, parents should consistently direct their children to use the toilet whenever they have to eliminate.

The use of a toilet schedule is a good way to help children get into the habit of using the adult toilet. Because schedules promote regular toilet usage, they have the additional benefit of helping accidents to occur with less frequency.

Instituting a toilet schedule is not difficult. Parents prompt children to use the restroom on a regular basis, such as about once an hour and also at key times (e.g., first thing in the morning, before bath time, after lunch, or before leaving the house). Simply asking children if they have to use the restroom at this point may not be enough, as children may not want to stop doing whatever fun activity they're participating in to go use the potty. Instead, adults need to phrase their request that children use the toilet as a non-optional command. Grandpa might say something like, "Tuttu, it's potty time. Let's go to the potty and see if we can hit the bullseye!"

Even with reminders and fun potty games built into the day, new toilet users will still have accidents. Parents need to be prepared for these accidents and plan in advance how to best respond to them. Clean clothes, baby wipes or a moist washcloth in a plastic zip-top bag, and empty gallon-sized zip-top bags should always be handy for a quick clean-up. Beds should be covered with water-resistant liners, and at first, children should still wear a diaper or disposable training pants while sleeping. As is the case throughout training, parents need to remain calm and matter-of-fact when accidents occur and try not to get frustrated or upset.

Accidents are completely normal during toilet training and should be expected occurrences. There are many possible causes for accidents. Some children will have not yet fully learned how to recognise their body's sensations warning of impending elimination need just yet. Other children may be distracted from focusing on toileting because they have become preoccupied, tired, excited, stressed, or are getting sick. It is also possible that children have developed an infection that is interfering with their toilet abilities. Children who continue to have lots of accidents or develop fever, pain during urination, or blood in the urine should be checked by doctor.

Bedwetting, Encopresis and Enuresis

Bedwetting

Children normally master the steps of toilet training tasks in a general developmental sequence. They typically first learn to notice the signals that they need to go to the bathroom and then how to react in time to handle waking or daytime defecation. It takes longer for children to learn how to handle night-time defecation (which occurs when they are sleeping). Next, children normally figure out how to react in time to their bodies' signals for daytime urination. Successfully managing night-time urination is the hardest task for young children to master, and as such, this step may take them the longest amount of time to achieve. Bedwetting is common challenge for families with preschool-aged children. Around 40 percent of 4-year-olds wet the bed several times a week. Nearly 20 percent of 5-year-olds and 10 percent of 6-year-olds have occasional accidents.

Night-time dryness is almost completely determined by children's degree of physiological (body) maturity. This means that in order for children to stay dry throughout the night, they first have to develop a bladder and muscle system which is large and strong enough to hold a full night's capacity of urine. This is complicated by the fact that children make even more urine throughout the night than they do during the day. Some children have the ability to wake up in the middle of the night to use the bathroom. However, the development of this capacity requires that children's brain mature to the point where they can receive and process bodily signals of impending urination and then wake up in time to make it to the bathroom. In general, the older children become, the more mature their brains are, and the more likely they are to develop this capacity.

While parents can't make their children mature faster, there are a few things they can do to help children make it through the night with fewer incidents. Parents can improve children's night-time dryness by limiting their fluid intake starting an hour or two before bed. This means that children should not drink lots of water, juice, soda, etc., shortly before bedtime.

Night-time pottying can be made easier if parents put a portable potty beside children's bedside for easier access. This is especially helpful during the early phases of toilet training when children may only have a few moments between waking and releasing. It is of lesser importance as children mature and can hold themselves back for longer periods of time. Night-lights can be placed at intervals between the bed and bathroom to make a night-time bathroom trip safer and less scary. For further reassurance, many small children will want to wake up Daddy or Mommy for assistance or for moral support. If possible, parents should continue to support this behaviour until children feel comfortable going to the bathroom on their own.

While it is tempting to rush children out of diapers and to promote their independent use of the adult toilet, parents really need to carefully consider whether their children are ready for this treatment. Night-time diapers or disposable training pants may need to be continued for a time, and should be if this decreases children's night-time accidents. Children are not generally ready to try sleeping through the night without the assistance of a diaper or training pant until they can stay dry for three to four hours between bathroom breaks during the day. Children who are ready to sleep without training pants will regularly wake up dry in the morning, or will demonstrate that they sometimes wake up in the night and use the bathroom. Children's readiness is not all purely physical either. If children seem scared or upset at the prospect of using underwear instead of training pants at night, it's a sign they are not emotionally ready for this step and parents should consider backing off for a time.

Even if a child shows all the signs that they are capable of going without a diaper through the night, parents should still ready themselves for the possibility of night-time accidents. Keeping a waterproof mattress pad on the bed is a smart move for all children up through the late elementary years, as it protects the mattress from night-time wetting accidents, night-time sickness, and bottles of juice that find their way into bed. As well, clean sheets and pyjamas should be kept within easy reach for a quick switch should that be necessary during the night. Older kids, around age six and up, can be taught to change their own sheets, pyjamas, and to put the dirty laundry into the designated hamper or storage area. Putting away your own dirty linens should be presented as just another responsibility people have for taking care of their own hygiene, and not as a punishment or discipline strategy. Parents should avoid making comments that are shaming when older children have accidents, and remain matter-of-fact and reassuring, just as is the case whenever any potty accident takes place.

The majority of children will have completed their toilet training by around ages 6 or 7. If bedwetting persists consistently until or past age 6 or 7, or if bedwetting is accompanied by other sleeping problems, parents should consult their family doctor. Moreover, if a child has had mostly dry nights for a long period of time and then suddenly regresses and develops a frequent bedwetting problem again, a doctor should also be notified. Bedwetting that does not resolve could be caused by an infection. Or, if the bedwetting is accompanied by nightmares or other fear reactions, there could be other emotional problems or situations at work. Bedwetting accompanied by fear can be a sign that abuse is taking place, for example.

Encopresis and Enuresis

Children who persistently have problems with soiling themselves may have Encopresis. Encopresis simply means that a child who is developmentally at least four years old regularly ends up pooping in inappropriate places, such as in clothing, or in bed during the night. The inappropriate defecation must occur at least once a month over a three or more month period, and can be voluntary or involuntary. It cannot be as a result of a medical condition, unless that medical condition includes constipation as a side effect. The term Encopresis is just a label that doctors and other clinicians use to describe an age-inappropriate soiling problem; it is not itself a source or cause of a soiling problem.

If children continue to have problems wetting themselves or wetting the bed beyond the developmental age of 5, their doctor may diagnose them with Enuresis. Enuresis is simply a label used to describe children who is at least five years old developmentally, and who regularly urinate in the wrong places or at the wrong time (whether involuntarily or on purpose). This regular urination problem must occur at least twice a week for three or more months in a row. A doctor may also diagnose Enuresis when children are wetting themselves less frequently but the behaviour is nevertheless creating significant emotional or social problems at school or home. Enuresis is not diagnosed when a medication or another medical condition is causing the wetting problem. As is the case with Encopresis, Enuresis is not a cause or reason why a wetting problem is occurring; it simply describes that occurrence of this sort of problem.

While hardly a simple task for small children to learn, toilet training doesn't have to be an overwhelming experience for children or for their parents. With a little knowledge, preparation, sensitivity, and creativity, a few tools and materials, and a whole lot of love, patience and enthusiasm, parents can help their little ones along the winding path towards their ultimate success as fully toilet trained children. Children's successful mastery of toilet training dramatically increases their independence, making it possible for them to attend school and community programmes and to interact with school-aged peers for extended periods of time.

How to Make Your Toddler go to Sleep?

As your toddler starts becoming more independent, it's tempting to think of him or her as "beyond babyhood", but keep in mind that your toddler still needs a lot of attention, a lot of cuddling, and a lot of sleep. If you regularly have to wake your toddler in the morning, it could be a sign that he or she isn't getting enough sleep.

Toddlers need between 12 and 14 hours of sleep in total—usually 11 to 12 hours at night and another one to three hours during the day.

Some parents decide to switch from a cot to a toddler bed at the two-year mark, especially if they need the cot for a new baby. But switching your toddler to a bed at too early an age could be disruptive and cause a setback. You may want to wait until your toddler is almost three years old before switching to a "big kid" bed.

If you need to do toddler sleep training with your toddler you are not alone. In her book *No Cry Sleep Solution for Toddlers and Pre-schoolers,* Elisabeth Pantley highlights that 70 per cent of parents with toddlers would change something about their child's sleep if they could. However, there's a lot you can do to minimise toddler sleep problems. For me, toddler sleep training begins from when your toddler first awakes and continues throughout the day right up until bedtime. If you want your toddler to sleep well at nights, then his activities, his routine, his daily naps and your presence all play a part. A toddler's bedtime routine is also extremely important to help your child drop off to sleep.

New Resources for Sleepy Babies

Your toddler's sleep patterns will change throughout the next year. For example, between one and two years, your toddler may give up his or her morning nap. And, although most toddlers will have learned to sleep through the night, change and stressful events (a trip, illness or new baby, for example) could cause temporary setbacks. If your toddler has just started daycare or preschool, his or her nap time may be shifted to accommodate the needs of the entire group of children. And because your toddler will need to get up at a set time each morning, it's especially important to ensure that he or she is getting enough sleep at night.

Create a Sleepy Time Routine

If you haven't already, now's the time to create a sleepy time routine that will help your toddler fall asleep on his or her own. If you follow the same pattern every evening, your child will feel more relaxed in knowing what's coming next. And try to keep regular nap times for your toddler. Restricting naps won't help your toddler sleep better at night. The daily routine is vital for toddler sleep training. It helps ensure that your child is tired enough to drop off to sleep quickly at bedtime.

— *Wake up time*. If you want your child to have an early bedtime it's best not to let them sleep too late. The wake up time of your child is very important because it will affect the time your toddler take his daily nap and therefore his bedtime. Obviously your timings may vary a little but if your child is sleeping until 8 a.m. or later it means their nap will be later and therefore bedtime is likely to be later than 7. p.m..

— *Daily activities*. Research has shown that children who are physically active take less time to fall to sleep. Therefore it's important that your toddler gets lots of physical activity throughout the day. Think trips to the park, the playground, soft play for toddlers, and swimming. Even a trip to a toddler group is stimulating and means your toddler will be wandering about playing with different toys. If you do things like shopping make sure your toddler gets a chance to walk about and isn't just sitting in a pushchair. If its raining and you're stuck in the house, put on some music and dance around or maybe do some active nursery rhymes such as head, shoulder, knees and toes. Try and get your toddler out and about during the day. Lots of exercise and fresh air is very helpful for a good nights sleep.

— *Naps*. Every toddler is different but many toddlers need or benefit from some kind of daytime nap until they are about 3 years old. Having a daytime nap helps toddlers to be alert, active and awake throughout the afternoon so that they have enough energy to tire themselves out for their night sleep. If a toddler doesn't have a nap there is a danger that they will over tire themselves and then find it hard to settle at night. Don't let your toddler nap too late as then they will not feel sleepy at bedtime. As a general rule toddlers of a 12 months to 2 years require 1 to 2 naps totalling 2 to 3 hours. A 2 year old requires at least 1 nap of about 1 to 2 hours. Some 3 year olds may even need up to an hour's nap. However, make sure your toddler doesn't get more sleep than he/she needs in the daytime.

Ideas for a Successful Night Sleep

Keep it short and sweet—20 to 45 minutes tops. Taking two hours to get ready for bed is not a night time routine, it's an evening activity! Keep your toddler's bedroom dark, cool, and quiet. A night-light is fine; a television isn't. Likewise, during the day, allow time for your toddler to wind down before nap time. Your toddler's routine should include three main steps:

1. A warm bath
2. A soothing massage and
3. Quiet time

Your night time routine can also include changing into pyjamas, reading books together, sharing a song, or whatever works best for your toddler. Save snuggle time, reading stories, or playing a special game for last. This will encourage your child to head right to bed.

How to Keep Toddlers Active?

Toddlers don't like to sit still. They wriggle from your grasp and want to be free. That's tiring for you, but it's a very good thing for them. Toddlers are naturally driven to do what is healthiest for them—be as active as possible much of their waking days. Children between the ages of 12 to 36 months old should get at least 30 minutes of structured physical activity (adult-led) and at least 60 minutes of unstructured physical activity (free play) every day. In addition, toddlers shouldn't be inactive for more than 1 hour at a time, except for sleeping.

At Home

You're in the driver's seat when you're the one taking care of your child. To limit sedentary time, don't let your child spend too much time in strollers, car seats, and high chairs. All these can keep kids from being active enough.

Limiting television is another good way to help keep your child physically active. TV, including videos and DVDs, is not recommended at all for kids under age 2. Those guidelines relax for older toddlers, but kids don't *need* to watch any TV. Even educational programmes aren't as enriching as real-life activities, such as figuring out how a toy works, playing games, or singing songs together.

If you choose to allow some TV time for your older toddler, try to follow this guideline: No more than 1 to 2 hours of quality children's programming per day. If possible, choose non-commercial TV because commercial TV exposes kids to food advertising, which often pushes low-nutrient snack foods and drinks. Another option is age-appropriate videos, especially those that invite kids to play along.

Away From Home

If your toddler spends time with a caregiver or at a childcare centre, it's important to investigate how much activity the kids get:

- Do they go outside most days?
- Is there a schedule of activities they adhere to?
- Do they watch videos or TV, and if so, how much and how often?

Another option is a playgroup, which is a great way to get kids together for some active time. A playgroup is also a welcome change of pace for stay-at-home parents, who benefit from the social time with other moms and dads. The parents could plan some time for structured group activities, such as playing a game, and let the kids do their own thing for some of the time. Meeting at a playground or large, indoor space is ideal.

If you've ever seen a group of toddlers playing, you may have noticed that they don't seem to be interacting as much as older kids do. Still, be assured they enjoy this time together. Eventually, they will start playing in more cooperative ways.

Provide a Safe Environment

Wherever a toddler is being active, the play area must be safe. At home, use gates and other safety equipment to make at least one room in the house safe enough for a toddler to explore. Away from home, look for childcare facilities and playgrounds that have newer, age-appropriate equipment that's not too big or challenging for your toddler. Also, ask about whether kids are separated by age—a practice that helps prevent injuries.

But no matter how "safe" the environment, there's no substitute for supervision. Many toddlers seem to subscribe to the "no fear" philosophy and may climb to the top of the monkey bars without reservation.

Close supervision is important because even though toddlers show improving skills, they lack sufficient balance, coordination, and judgement. In other words, keep a close eye and be there to catch them!

Encourage Activity

It might look like just child's play, but toddlers are hard at work learning important physical skills as they gain muscle control, balance, and coordination. Each new skill lets them progress to the next one, building on a foundation that leads to more complicated physical tasks, such as jumping rope, kicking a ball on the run, or turning a cartwheel. Toddlers always want to do more, which can motivate them to keep trying until they acquire a new skill, no matter what it takes. Take advantage of your toddler's natural desire to keep moving. Even at this early age, kids establish patterns of activity that carry through the rest of childhood. So an active toddler is likely to remain active later.

Developing Skills

Playing and learning are completely natural for toddlers, so mastering the skills below should be fun and games for them. Parents should give toddlers many opportunities to practice their developing skills while providing supervision so they stay safe while they learn. In addition to these physical accomplishments, toddlers are developing in other ways. Provide opportunities for yours to explore, ask questions, use his or her imagination, and practice fine motor skills, such as stacking blocks or colouring. Here is some guidelines to the physical skills toddlers are working, by age:

Early Toddler Skills (12-24 months)

- Walks independently.
- Pulls/carries toys while walking.
- Stoops and gets back up.
- Begins to run.
- Kicks a ball.

— Holds railing up/down stairs.

— Walks backward.

Older Toddler Skills (24-36 months)

— Balances 1 to 2 seconds on one foot.

— Climbs well.

— Bends over easily without falling.

— Runs well.

— Kicks ball forward.

— Both feet on step, up and down stairs.

— Starts to pedal tricycle.

— Throws ball over head.

Types of Daily Activities

Children of 12-36 months old should have following types of daily activities:

— At least 30 minutes of structured physical activity (adult-led).

— At least 60 minutes unstructured physical activity (free play).

As a general rule, toddlers shouldn't be inactive for more than 1 hour at a time, except for sleeping. That's a lot of work for parents and caregivers, but a lot of much-needed activity for toddlers. Encourage your toddler to be active, and remember how much he or she is learning along the way.

Toddler Discipline

Toddler discipline is a very difficult task for parents. As parents, we would need to set limits and provide structure to create an atmosphere in the home that makes these limits easier to respect. One of the developmental tasks that toddlers undergo is looking and testing for boundaries. As such, it is important that they clearly know where these boundaries lie. They must also learn that there is consistency in the way that these behaviours are handled when they cross the boundaries. When you first implement structure, you can expect A lot of testing, crying and often an increase in misbehaviours as they will be testing your limits.

Discipline is grounded on a healthy relationship between parent and child. To know how to discipline your child you must first know your child. Build and strengthen this connection between you and your child and this will lay the foundation for discipline. Once your child trusts you to meet her needs, she will trust you to set her limits.

The following lists out some ways for toddler discipline:

Time Out

This is one of the most common toddler discipline method. Keep the time brief around one minute per year of age. Toddlers don't usually stay in the corner so it means stopping what you are doing and standing over them with your side or back to them so that they can't engage your facial/body language. Once time out is over, you can remind them what they did wrong in very simple language and then if they do it again (as most toddlers will immediately do upon being released from time out until they have the concept) they go back into the corner. Discipline must occur at the time of the action and not an hour or longer after. So even if you are out of your home, you must be prepared to discipline them. Be discreet, and remember always not to do it in front of others to avoid bringing down his self-esteem. Remind toddlers of the rules frequently when out on an outing or in the house if necessary.

Distract and Divert

The best form of toddler discipline is redirection. First, you have to distract them from their original intention and then, quickly divert them toward a safer alternative. Give them something else to do for example, helping with the household chores and soon they will be enjoying themselves rather than investing a lot of emotional energy into the original plan.

Ignoring Temper Tantrum

Ignoring the behaviour or making statements such as when you throw a tantrum I can't hear you or I don't like watching temper tantrums so let me know when you are finished and we will talk, will both show and tell the child that their display of temper tantrums will not gain them control over the situation or the parent.

Temper tantrums are usually dramatic, intense and full of emotion. With a little practice and persistence, parents can learn how to stop the drama of a temper tantrum and change the situation to a calm, quiet discussion. Keep control and keep the peace.

Encourage Cooperation

Your child is more likely to do what you say if you uses soft approaches like these—Ask rather than tell. Say "Would you give me the book, please?" instead of demanding "Bring me the book."

Set Limits

Much of your toddler discipline depends upon your ability to set limits. Boundaries provide security for the child whose adventurous spirit leads him to explore, but his inexperience may lead him astray. For example, your toddler doesn't want to hold your hand as you cross a street or parking lot together. You firmly set a limit: street or parking lot crossing is only done while holding hands. There is no option. We need to achieve the right balance between freedom and constraints for our toddlers.

Limit-setting teaches a valuable lesson for life: the world is full of yeses and nos. You decide what behaviour you cannot allow and stick to that limit. This will be different for each family and each stage of development. Toddlers want someone to set limits. It makes them feel secure and loved, and helps them to understand boundaries. As a parent you have to ensure that the rules you set are simple, easy to understand, and consistent.

Provide Structure

Set-up conditions for toddler discipline that encourage desirable behaviour to happen. Structure protects and redirects. You free the child to be a child and provide the opportunity to grow and mature. Structure creates a positive environment for the child. By a bit of pre-planning you remove most of the "no's" so that a generally "yes" environment prevails.

Structure changes as the child grows. At all developmental levels restructuring the child's environment is one of your most valuable discipline strategies. When your infant reaches the grabby stage, you are careful to set your coffee cup out of his reach. When your toddler discovers the toilet, you start keeping the lid latched or the bathroom door closed. The pre-schooler who fights going to sleep at night gets a relaxing bedtime routine. The nine-year-old struggling to keep up with her homework gets a quiet, enticing place to work in, as well as firm restrictions on school-night television. Structure sets the stage for desirable behaviours to override undesirable ones.

Positive Reinforcement

Studies show that toddler discipline using positive reinforcement works far better than punishment. Rather than focusing only on those things that irritate us and becoming habitual scolders, "catch your kids doing something right and reward them."

Remember that toddlers tune out a lot so if you are always saying "No", "Don't touch this", "Don't go there", then all they hear is NO. You want to try and give them lots of positive feedback. Examples of positive feedback are to let them know they did a 'nice job following directions' or 'good job playing', with lots of hugs and kisses. Try using other "No" words like stop. You don't need to yell but you do need to put firmness 'don't mess with me' tone in your voice.

There is certainly no magic formula to toddler discipline but it is imperative that you establish the guidelines for behaviour in your house as quickly as possible. Whatever you do, make sure you are consistent in your toddler discipline. If you tell a child no and then eventually end up letting the child do what he wanted in the first place, you are setting yourself up for disaster. Even if you have changed your mind and decided that what the child was doing wasn't so bad after all, you need to stick to your decision and let the child know that you mean what you say. If he gets his way after a minute or after an hour, he will know he's got you pegged. As such, the key to toddler discipline is consistency.

6

Parenting of Young Children

One of the greatest joys in life is having a child in the house. Everyday, something new and exciting happens. However, one of the greatest challenges in life is the parenting that goes along with raising a young child. Proper parenting is crucial to keeping your child not only happy, but also safe, good parenting will teach your child important life lessons, guiding him or her into a stable, happy, and successful adulthood.

Realise that you will be faced with challenges, days where you feel you cannot go on, but you can and you will. With a lot of patience, the right attitude, and having some helpful tips to follow, you will find that parenting a young child is not so difficult. Remember, toddlers and younger kids are high energy, inquisitive, and manipulative. They know the buttons to push to get a reaction out of mom or dad. However, you will find these coping tools beneficial, actually allowing you to enjoy the parenting process instead of dreading it.

In the position of being a parent, you are a life coach, not a judge and jury. Your role involve providing your younger child with encouragement, guidance, and praise, along with high expectations, constructive criticism, and limitations. Typically, a child will accept the role of coach much better than judge or even parent. Judging a child will only cause him or her to pull away, which is something you want to avoid at all costs.

Although parenting young children does involve discipline, you will find that keeping the focus on the positive, the child's sensitivity, hard work, intelligence, caring attitude, and other good qualities will build self-confidence and develop a more willing spirit in the child to mind. There is nothing wrong with setting high expectations for younger children. This means establishing from an early age that you expect for him or her to get good grades, to graduate from high school, to choose friends wisely, and so on.

Some parents feel that competition is a bad thing but actually, healthy competition is good. Actually, parenting young children and teaching them health competition choices does not mean placing the emphasis on always winning, but instead, of always doing his or her best, not allowing another person to win. Over time, the younger child will gain a new sense of confidence and character. Each child has to find his or her own way in social settings. If your child does not fit in with a particular group, the "in crowd", do not pressure. Every child has his or her own "in crowd" and as long as the friends are good, support their choice.

Nurturing is vital to children's development, a secret ingredient that enables children to grow physically, mentally, socially, emotionally, culturally, and spiritually. It doesn't matter if children are provided with a healthy diet, adequate shelter and medical care. If they are not adequately nurtured as well, their health and development will generally suffer. It's a good thing, then, that nurturing children is one of the more fun and rewarding parts of raising a family. Nurture activities allow parents to express their creative, loving, and playful sides as they help their children grow and learn.

There is no one single and proper way to nurture a child. Some parents, anxious to do their best, worry that they may not be adequately nurturing their children, or that they may not be nurturing their children the "right way". For the most part, such concerns are unfounded. By its nature nurturing is a creative and spontaneous activity that can take many forms. Most any activity parents engage in that shows children that they are loved will be an effective act of nurture. It is important that parents encourage and select nurturing activities that will help young children to develop properly, but in most cases, parents will naturally and spontaneously be drawn to select and provide children with nurturing activities that will accomplish this goal.

Food and Nutrition for Young Children

Young children need a balanced and healthy diet to fuel the amazing rate of growth and development that occurs during early childhood. For better or for worse, after age 2, young children eat many of the same foods adults eat. As a result, it's important that caregivers provide children with a menu that includes a variety of nutrient-dense choices from all important food groups. Caregivers should also take care to minimise children's access to "junk foods" that are low in nutrient value and high in sugar, fat, and salt.

Adults and children over the age of two need to eat a daily diet that consists of whole grains, fruits, vegetables, lean protein, calcium-rich dairy products, and some oils. Whole grains are important because they retain dietary fibre, and naturally occurring oil, vitamins and minerals that have been removed from more refined grains like white flour. For example, bread made with 100 per cent whole wheat flour is more nutritionally sound than bread made with refined white flour because the latter has had the healthy bran fibre and natural wheat oil removed during the refining process. In general, whole-grain selections, such as bread, crackers or pasta made with 100 per cent whole wheat, brown rice and oatmeal, will be significantly higher in fibre and important nutrients than white bread, white rice and other refined grain products.

Children can choose from a wide array of fruits and vegetables in the produce section of the grocery store. Selecting fruits and vegetables based on their colour makes for an easy rule of thumb; select fruits and vegetables with dark and vibrant colours because these colours indicate the presence of large amounts of vitamins and minerals. Dark green (e.g., spinach) and dark orange (e.g., carrots) vegetables are especially nutritionally valuable. Healthy preparation of veggies is also important. Raw or lightly-steamed vegetables will generally contain more nutrients than fried vegetables, because too much heat can destroy some nutrients. In addition, frying veggies in oil adds additional fat and calories to these foods.

Because young children are still learning to perfect the biting, chewing, and swallowing process, caregivers need to take care to serve fruits and vegetables that have been cut up into small pieces, to prevent choking. As well, slightly cooking or steaming vegetables softens them and reduces choking risk.

Protein menu selections can include lean meats (e.g., chicken, turkey, or fish) as well as chickpeas, beans, and nuts. As with fruit and vegetables, caregivers need to carefully prepare protein-rich foods by cutting items into small pieces so as to minimise choking risk. As another choking precaution, very young children should avoid eating whole nuts and eat nut butters instead. A thin layer of a low-fat nut butter on whole-grain toast is an excellent kid-friendly protein selection. Be careful, though... a child who swallows a large glob of peanut butter sandwich can still easily choke.

Young children should get two to three servings of milk products each day. Milk selections can include two percent or skim milk, non-fat or low-fat yogurt (try freezing portable yogurt tubes for a special treat), or cheese. Milk products are filled with calcium, which is especially important in the early childhood stage, as bones are rapidly growing.

Lastly, children benefit from a little healthy oil or fat every day. Some fats are healthier than others. Eaten in moderation, polyunsaturated fats (found in safflower, sunflower, sesame, corn, and soy oils; and nuts and seeds) and mono-unsaturated fats (found in olives, avocados; and olive, canola, and peanut oils) can help reduce blood cholesterol levels and protect against heart disease. Omega-3 fatty acids (found in fish such as mackerel and salmon, flaxseed, and walnuts) can help lower blood pressure, control inflammation, and protect against irregular heartbeat. These healthy fats can be contrasted with various forms of saturated fat (red meat, milk, butter and cheese) which tend to cause health problems.

Young children (just like adults) need plenty of water to stay hydrated. When they are babies, children get most of their hydration from breast milk or formula. As children grow older and move away from breast and bottle feedings, it's appropriate to provide them with a non-spill "sippy" cup (or regular cup when appropriate) filled with water or milk at meals and throughout the day to encourage them to drink.

Parents should also monitor how much their children eat, and watch portion sizes. Young children's stomachs are relatively small, so they should consume smaller portions. Particularly at restaurants, modern people routinely consume servings that are "supersized." Therefore, children should be taught to listen to their bodies, and eat only until they are full. Encouraging children to clean their plate when they have an oversized portion in front of them is not healthy. Caregivers can help by not placing too much food on a child's plate, or requesting that restaurants package half of large portions in "to go" containers.

Because young children do not eat as much as adults at one sitting, they frequently need to nibble on snacks between meals. Caregivers should treat snacks as nutritious mini-meals, rather than as an excuse to fill up on sugary and/or fatty items. As with all food choices, the least processed foods are generally the healthiest to serve. Cut up fruit or veggies will be healthier for children than a piece of candy or a pile of chips.

Many parents may look at the above menu and sigh with a combination of wistfulness and frustration, knowing that their children are far from ideal eaters and might reject some of these choices. The key is to do what you can to tailor a healthy diet that capitalises on what your child will eat. Experiment and mix and match healthy choices within the different food groups to create meals that are appealing and nutritious.

The best way for caregivers to teach young children about nutrition is to make healthy eating part of your family's regular everyday lifestyle. Caregivers should themselves cook nutritious meals, sip on healthy beverages, and nibble on healthful snacks. Unfortunately, caregivers aren't the only influences in a young child's world. Kids will see cheese doodles, sugary cereals, and chocolate cupcakes on television or in grocery store displays. They will also inevitably sit next to or play with other children who eat a mind-boggling array of unhealthy junk foods. Caregivers should continue to model and encourage their children to engage in positive eating habits by making healthy choices at the store, restaurants, and friend's homes. Neither children nor adults should be eating salty fried snacks, fat and sugar-loaded sweets, caffeinated soft drinks, or greasy fast food as part of their daily menu. However, it's alright for caregivers to provide an occasional treat or splurge for their children. Allowing such treats teaches young children an important lesson from an early age that there are no bad or forbidden foods. Allowing all desired foods to be consumed (if in small portions and only occasionally) helps to defend children (especially little girls) from developing eating disorders later on in life.

If young children learn to like healthful foods and to make wise eating choices early on, they will be more likely to continue healthy eating behaviour in adulthood and consequently to become healthier adults. Healthy eating, combined with adequate exercise, can protect young children from developing obesity.

Children who are obese run the risk of developing social and emotional problems. For example, obese children are often ostracised or become the targets of bullies. These children may feel isolated and lonely, develop low self-esteem, and become anxious or depressed. In addition, children who are obese run a high risk of staying obese as adults. Adult obesity can lead to a host of additional health problems such as diabetes, cancer, stroke, and heart disease.

Obesity can often be prevented in today's youth by educating them about positive lifestyle habits, along with offering encouragement and guidance. If children start to become overweight and/or obese, take action as soon as possible. Seeking professional guidance is a good idea, as there are ways to help children regain a normal weight without using dieting strategies that are physically unhealthy and mentally damaging. Caregivers should consult with a pediatrician for any concerns about a child's eating behaviour and nutrition habits.

Beyond just providing the fuel and nutrients for growing up healthy, eating can also be an activity that promotes social development and family bonding. If family meal times are enjoyable events that encourage talking, sharing, and laughing, young children will be eager to participate and to become part of the action. This will also help young children feel connected, loved, and part of the family. Moreover, they can begin to learn basic manners and social rules. By watching other adults and children at the dinner act respectfully by saying "please" and "thank you" (and using other appropriate table manners) they will gradually learn polite table manners too. It's important for caregivers to remember that young children are in the process of learning the rules, and don't yet have them perfected. Too much insistence on proper form, or harshness when manners are temporarily forgotten can be counter-productive. The goal is to create a family culture involving meals that are relaxed and fun for youngsters and other participants, rather than an anxious or argumentative time.

Caregivers shouldn't attempt to force new foods on young children who aren't open to them. However, by giving children multiple chances to try these foods across multiple meals, children may gradually become tempted to be more adventurous eaters. Some parents may be tempted to bribe young children to try a new healthful food by promising a special sweet reward at the end of the meal. This may get the child to comply in the short term, but over time this method tends to teach children to seek bribes (increasing amounts of reward) rather than to seek out new experiences for their own sake.

Creating Nurturing Space in Early Childhood

Creating nurturing spaces isn't just about clearing out some room in the basement for a playroom. "Space" in this sense includes not only the physical area and objects for playing and learning, but also encompasses the time, attitude, and energy necessary for creating nurturing child-parent interactions.

Each home should have a physical space that can be used for play time. Every home is different, and many will not be large enough to have an entire room dedicated to play. That's OK. The kitchen table can be a perfect place for craft and other hands-on activities when it's not being used for serving a meal. Empty space on the floor in the living room can be an ideal place for make-believe or for a puppet show. A parent's bed can be ideal for quiet time reading, singing, or snuggling.

It is important to dedicate whatever space is to be used for play to the task of play, at least during play times. Dedicating an area to play means that other clutter or objects are moved out of the way to create room for the activity that's going to happen. It also means that other potential distractions need to be removed or turned off (e.g., magazines, TV, the cell phone). Creating a dedicated play space sends a message to young children that play activity is important. The space can be restored to its regular use (as a living room or kitchen table, etc.) after play time is over.

In addition to dedicating a play space, it is also important to dedicate a regular play time during which a parent's attention will be fully focused on nurturing interactions. While today's parents have many life responsibilities and often must multi-task to get everything done, every effort should be made to preserve a few times during the week when children can receive their parent's full attention. Parents can be more truly physically, mentally, and emotionally present for their children when they aren't trying to do other things at the same time. Games are more fun when the players are not waiting for a person who is ironing clothes between turns or repeatedly answering cell phone calls.

Nurturing opportunities are concentrated during special play times, but are not limited to them. Nurturing opportunities may present themselves at many different places and times. Standing in line at the grocery store might be the perfect time and place for a parent and children to share a special game or song. This way, children are still learning, growing, and having fun, and mother's sanity is saved by the absence of crying and whining all the way past the chocolate bars. Similarly, running an errand can serve double duty as a time to sing silly songs together, or for children to point out colours, letters, and shapes that they see. Something as mundane as going to pick up dry cleaning can become a fun (and educational) experience if parents approach it with love, humour and creativity.

Physical Nurturing

Pre-operational aged children continue to work on mastering and refining a wide range of gross and fine motor skills. Parents can help encourage children's physical growth and development by promoting activities that require children to display increasing levels of physical strength and skill.

Gross Motor Activities

Gross motor skills involve large-body movements. With practice, kids can build speed, balance, endurance, and the more sophisticated levels of coordination necessary to master new physical activities, such as bicycle riding, roller skating, dancing, swimming, swinging on a jungle gym, and team sports such as baseball, soccer, and basketball. Beyond honing physical abilities, parental encouragement of physical activity will also instill a love of physical fitness (and health) that can continue through adulthood. Most complex activities children try will seem difficult at first, and require lots of patience and practice to master. Parents can be both teachers and cheerleaders; modelling how to swing a baseball or balance on a bicycle, as well as encouraging their children as they inevitably fall and must start over again.

Most young kids enjoy learning how to balance and to move on wheeled toys such as tricycles, bicycles, roller skates and skateboards. Most will also enjoy learning new sports, when games are modified for their skill and ability levels. Children who are learning to play baseball can use light, plastic "whiffle" balls with holes in them and similarly light plastic bats. These balls and bats are easier and safer for children to throw and catch and will hurt less should an accident occur. Parents can mount standard size basketball hoops low down to the ground or improvise a basketball hoop by placing a kid-friendly ring at an appropriate level on the garage door or shed wall. The use of squishy "Nerf" balls, smaller playing fields, and a no-tackle rule can also help adapt games like soccer and football so that little children can play them safely.

Kids can even practice a safe form of preschool archery. Parents can paint a large bulls-eye on a piece of old cardboard and hang it from a sturdy tree limb. Children can then throw bean bags at the bulls-eye to improve their throwing skills and hand-eye coordination. A bean bag toss is another activity that helps hand-eye coordination. Parents can cut the bottom ends off gallon plastic milk jugs, and kids can practice with a partner catching and throwing the bags in the jugs.

Parents can also consider signing children up for physical activities or team sports outside the home. Children's participation on such teams helps foster their development of social and teamwork skills such as taking turns, following instructions, and working toward a common goal. Children can join a soccer, T-ball, or basketball team at the local community or recreation centre. Alternatively, children can take swimming lessons, join a swim team, or enrol in music and movement, tumbling, gymnastics, ballet, karate, tap dance, hip-hop, or other physical education classes at local recreation centers or dance schools. Many communities feature a wide variety of children's activities at a relatively low cost. In some areas, lower income families can apply for scholarships to subsidize their children's participation.

When parents nurture young children's fine motor skills, they are encouraging activities that develop hand-eye coordination and other smaller hand skills such as drawing, cutting, and crafting. Parents can offer children a large range of tools to encourage fine motor skills and creativity, such as crayons, paint, glue, building blocks, blunt scissors, magazines, construction paper, play clay, ribbons, cloth, buttons, sand, beads, water, etc. Encouraging fine motor development can be as easy as giving kids some of these materials and letting them construct whatever they like. However, parents can also provide general instructions for completing a particular project and in so doing, encourage children to develop new skills that they have not seen nor tried before.

"Sewing" can be another fun activity that will help small children refine their fine motor skills while enhancing their artistic talents. For young toddlers, parents can cut out large shapes (e.g., animals, geometric, or seasonal items) from pieces of cardboard and then punch holes around the perimeter of these shapes with a hole punch. Kids can then lace yarn or string from hole to hole around the perimeter of each shape until the shapes are surrounded. Older pre-schoolers and younger school-aged children can use inexpensive large-gage plastic mesh sheets (found in most craft stores) as the base on which to stitch designs and patterns using different colored yarn and blunted plastic needles made especially for this activity.

Yet another domestic activity that will booster hand-eye coordination and creativity is cookie decorating. Large sugar cookies, some colourful icing, some sprinkles, and some clean paint brushes make for a fun and edible craft. This can be an especially fun activity around birthdays or special holidays, as children can easily make a gift to present to Grandma, Daddy, a teacher, or someone else that is special in their lives. It's fun for children to mix and roll dough, but make sure they are kept away from the hot oven and hot cookie sheets!

Parents must supervise all of children's fine-motor play activities and assume responsibility for making sure children remain safe. Parents need to make sure that they're providing children with safe and child-friendly craft materials, such as blunt scissors, non-toxic, lead-free paints and glues, etc. Small children under the age of three years shouldn't be given beads, glitter, or other craft materials that could pose a choking hazard. No matter the child, material, or project, parents should always be providing supervision so as to ensure that safe decisions are made and to intervene if necessary.

Cognitive Nurturing

Parents can encourage activities that enhance young children's mental development. Pre-operational children (ages 2 to 7 years) learn in a very concrete, hands-on manner, so direct play and interaction are the best vehicles for teaching them concepts. There are many fun concrete skills children can practice to expand their concentration, memory, abstract thinking and decision-making abilities.

Age-appropriate puzzles are fun challenges that encourage problem-solving and critical thinking skills. Simple board games can also encourage problem-solving skills as well as teach young children how to follow a set of directions. In addition, games and puzzles can help teach categorisation, concentration and memory skills. As children grow, the rules and objectives of the games they play can become more complicated and interesting. Classic games like Checkers are good to introduce at this time. Many fun puzzles and board games can be purchased in the store, but families can also easily make their own. For example, extra photos or large magazine pictures can be covered with clear plastic contact paper and then cut into large, irregular shapes to make jigsaw puzzles.

Throughout the pre-operational period, young children continue to benefit from make-believe play. By creating their own imaginary setting and placing themselves within it, kids learn to stretch their imagination and creative thinking skills. Most children spontaneously play games of "pretend" in which they act like something other than themselves, like a dinosaur, or a princess. Though such games may not make sense to parents, children will still generally benefit from playing them. Parents can encourage such make-believe play by simply jumping into the game as best they can. Many children will be in total glee that their parents are playing along. However, some children have an internalised set of directions or beliefs surrounding their make-believe scene and will promptly correct any adult who doesn't play by these hidden rules that seem so obvious to them. So long as children aren't hitting or screaming to make their point, parents should just play along and adjust to their child's creative train of thought as best they can.

When children are out of ideas themselves, parents can take a turn creating the make-believe setting and encourage the little ones to play along. Parents' make-believe play can be as silly and off-the-wall as what their children come up with, or it can be more structured in nature so as to provide lessons about specific topics. Themes for adult-driven make-believe play can include nurturing and caring scenes (such as taking care of a baby or playing house) or rough and tumble, interactive scenes (such as playing good guys vs. bad guys, or pretending to be a wild animal). Parents should encourage a variety of different forms of play (even if they're not always excited to play all varieties themselves). So long as play themes are not violent or hurtful, they are likely okay.

Early childhood years are a perfect time for adults to nurture children's musical and creative interests. Young children love to create musical rhythms as well as to listen to music on the radio, TV or MP3 player. They also love to sing and to watch child-friendly live performances. There are many toy instruments designed to accommodate children's small bodies that allow them to make musical sound with minimal coordination. However, parents can also make instruments. Any pot or pan can be a drum. Boxes or other closed vessels (e.g., oatmeal containers filled with dry rice) are perfect shakers. Strings stretched over a hole in the lid of a shoe box make a great primitive guitar.

Young children can make whatever sound combinations they'd like on their instruments, but parents can also guide and encourage the repetition of simple rhythms and sounds. Parents can also teach children simple songs that can be sung to background recordings, live instruments, or alone. If adult family members regularly play musical instruments such as the guitar or piano, adults can encourage children to sing along or to try playing the instrument themselves (with guidance, particularly if the instruments are delicate!). Whether parents are musical whizzes or they just sing off-key in the shower, children will love singing right along beside them.

Nurturing a child's love of reading does not need to involve books exclusively. There are lots of other activities and games that can encourage word and number literacy. Parents of toddlers can encourage storytelling, for instance. Parents can show children pictures in books or magazines and ask them to create relevant stories featuring these characters. This sort of creative exercise can be hard for toddlers to do without assistance, so parents can help them along by filling in details as cued by children's basic story ideas. Large felt boards with "stick on" cut-out people, animals, buildings, and background scenery can become a perfect interactive tool to help children visualise and practice story-telling. Commercial felt boards can be expensive, but crafty families can make their own with a piece of plywood, lots of felt material, and a little cutting skill. Parents of older children can encourage story collage creation. After reading or hearing a story, children can cut out and assemble pictures from old magazines that remind them of related story details, characters, or settings.

Young school-aged children can work on counting in multiples (e.g., counting by 10's or 100's), as well as adding and subtracting. Give children 100 beans, chocolate candies, pennies, or other small objects, and 10 cups. Have the children arrange the objects into groups of 10, and then put each of those groups into the cups. Ask them to finish by counting cups. This game, which helps children learn to visualise number problems, can be extended for use with groups of 20, 25, or any other multiple number. The game can be made more complicated by supplying an odd number of objects so as to illustrate the concept of a remainder. Children can graduate from this counting game to more complex games, such as a money-handling "store" game where they must set prices for items sold in an imaginary store, "buy" those items and then give themselves accurate change.

Another fun way that children can learn while playing is through at-home science experiments. Parents can design safe, age-appropriate and stimulating interactive activities that help children to learn concepts like measurement, cause and effect, gravity and the life cycle. As is the case with many academic topics, fostering children's early interest in science tends to pay off in their continuing interest as they grow. Science demonstrations are more complicated than most reading or math exercises. Therefore, parents frequently need to supervise these activities more closely than others if planned outcomes are to happen.

Social Nurturing

Many types of nurturing can be encouraged through one-on-one parent-child activities, such as riding bicycles, doing crafts, reading, playing games or puzzles, or playing instruments. However, activities designed to foster children's social development requires their involvement with other people, both children and adults. Parents can help encourage socialisation by planning opportunities for children to interact with their peers. Socialisation activities need not be complex in nature. A simple trip to the park or playground at a time when these locations are likely to be busy creates an opportunity for children to interact spontaneously with peers. Alternatively, parents can organise formal play-dates that allow specific children to play together at specific places.

Typically, the less parents try to direct children's socialisation, the better that socialisation goes. When parents remove themselves from dictating these social interactions, it forces children to learn how to communicate, to share, to negotiate, and to solve their own disagreements. Such an open approach does not work well for all children, however. Some children are very shy and need a fair amount of encouragement before they will engage with peers. For these children, parents should arrange play-dates where fewer children are present. Parents who have shy children may also need to assume an active initiatory role to help get the play started, so as to allow time for everyone to feel safe and comfortable. As children begin to have fun on their own, parents can gradually fade into the background.

Beyond helping kids develop strong social bonds with peers, parents should also encourage family and sibling bonding. Siblings may be spaced far apart in age, or have very different interests and abilities; therefore, parents may need to be extra creative in order to come up with activities that everyone will enjoy. Siblings should be encouraged to resolve their own conflicts whenever possible, as this will tend to reduce sibling rivalry over time and build stronger sibling bonds. However, parents should not become so "hands-off" that they ignore sibling interactions that are violent, intimidating, or cruel. In these cases, adults should intervene as soon as possible.

Families can also build traditions by establishing regular activities (e.g., nightly family meals, Friday night movie nights, Tuesday night game nights, or family bike rides on the weekends) that the entire family does together. Creating activities in which children can interact with extended family (e.g., cousins, grandparents, aunts, and uncles) allows them to build close relationships with these extended family members, and helps them to establish a sense of history and identity. It is much easier to foster a sense of extended family closeness when family members live near to one another. However, even when extended family members are spread across states or the entire country, regular telephone calls or web video sessions over the internet can be coordinated to keep the family spirit alive.

Young children need to be reminded, encouraged, and rewarded for practicing proper social manners. How far to take this social learning is up to individual parents. Different families put different values on how formally their members should conduct themselves with regard to manners. However, common courtesies (including phrases like "Thank you" and "Excuse me", and practices like sending a thank you card after receiving a gift) are universal and should be taught to all children.

Emotional Nurturing

Children's emotional development is harder to visualise and to measure than are other aspects of development. However, it is no less important than other forms of development, and in many ways is key. Children's emotional maturation provides a foundation upon which social developments may take place. Parents encourage children's emotional development by expressing their unconditional love and affection, by helping children to feel special and valued, and by helping them learn to understand their emotions and feelings.

One of the most valuable ways that parents can encourage healthy emotional development is by showing their children unconditional love and affection every day. Parents need to illustrate to their children that they appreciate and value them, and enjoy their company just because of who they are. The easiest ways that parents can express this love are through physical gestures of affection. Hugs, kisses, gentle "rough and tumble" play, gentle tickling, and snuggling in quiet moments are all wonderful ways parents can show love. Appropriate physical contact is still a vital ingredient of child development during the preschool years.

Parents can also use language to bond emotionally with their children. Kind nicknames that kids enjoy and which make them feel special, like "peanut" or "sweet pea" offer one verbal way of creating emotional intimacy. As well, offering words of encouragement and praise to children involved in activities is also beneficial. Finally, speaking the words "I love you" regularly also remind young children how parents feel about them.

It is also important to encourage children's increased understanding of emotions and the connection between thoughts, feelings, and actions during the pre-operational years. Parents can plan activities that help children to examine and understand the range of human emotions, as well as how such emotions can be read in people's faces. For example, parents can point out pictures of people feeling different emotions in magazines. Older children can draw or paint emotion faces out of paper plates and craft supplies. Parents can also play a game with children where they are encouraged to act out the different emotions a favourite character in a story experiences. Children's puppet shows and plays can also be wonderful vehicles for helping children act out and understand their own emotions as well as how others feel.

Parents can be instrumental in helping young children start to make connections between how they feel emotionally and physically. Adults can help children connect feelings and thoughts with actions, facial expressions, and body posture by making observations like this one: "Andy, I see you're scowling and clenching your fists. You look angry. What's going on?" Another fun and silly way to help young children make connections between how they feel and what they look like is to have them practice making emotion faces in the mirror.

Cultural Nurturing

Children are more likely to become adults who identify with their cultural and spiritual heritage if they grow up feeling included in cultural and spiritual communities. Parents can take an active role in shaping children's cultural and spiritual life by providing them with frequent opportunities to interact with peers and adults of all ages who share children's heritage or belief system, or who can otherwise function as cultural role models. Young children who see others practicing the same customs and rituals as they do themselves will feel a sense of belonging and pride.

Young children are very concrete. They learn through their direct experience and through observation of other's behaviour, and not by way of abstract discussion. It is of little use to explain the philosophical, historical or religious basis for a given cultural or spiritual practice to young children. Instead, children will best learn particular practices by participating in them. Religious or traditional cultural festivals, holidays, and rituals are perfect teaching opportunities, as are opportunities to teach children about traditional foods and dress. Children's participation in holidays and rituals and cultural activities teaches them that they are valued members of a particular community. Such memories form the ongoing basis of children's cultural and religious identity, and become the building blocks of tradition.

Besides immersing children in the ongoing practice of cultural and religious traditions, parents can also foster children's appreciation of their heritage through celebratory games and crafts. For instance, children may enjoy making books about historical family members or filling out a family tree so as to learn about grandma's mother and father. Children can also be encouraged to make scrapbooks documenting their participation in family occasions, and special cultural or religious celebrations. Filling the pages of home-made books with special photographs, drawings, labels, and short stories will help children create cherished keepsakes that reinforce their familial, cultural and religious identity. Making family movies or videos can achieve a similar effect. Though learning about one's own culture is paramount, it is also important to teach children about other people's cultures. Neighbours, family friends, and school peers can be recruited to help teach small children about other cultural practices including music, language, food and dress. Exposing children to other cultures at an early age helps develop their tolerance and appreciation of cultural differences and diversity; skills they will need to navigate the complex and culturally interdependent modern world.

Fostering Moral Behaviour in Children

With rising youth violence, increasing peer cruelty, coarsening of language, a declining work ethic, diminished personal and civic responsibility, escalating dishonesty, growing ethical illiteracy, and growing disrespect for parents, teachers, and other legitimate authority figures, one wonders if too little emphasis is placed on morality among the young. According to a number of scholars, the answer is a definitive yes.

Among the most vocal and widely respected of these voices is Harvard professor Robert Coles, author of *The Moral Intelligence of Children*. Coles claims that at one time society took for granted its responsibility to help children develop a conscience or moral compass. But increasingly, "we notice [conscience] is less and less a force in the mental life of our children." Coles argues that society has stressed "cognitive competence of a certain kind," such as doing well in math and science. And then, he says, "We emphasised that elusive quality called mental health, psychological expressiveness, knowledge of one's emotional life. What are we going to do with all this awareness and competence? And for what moral purpose? I think that has not been stressed as much in many homes."

Moral intelligence is how we behave. It's moral behaviour tested by life and lived out in everyday experience, says Coles. The development of moral intelligence is critical if we are to have a moral society. How can we foster moral intelligence in our children? Coles believes one way is to tell them stories. In his book, he tells stories from his personal and professional life that examine "good" and "bad" children and how they became that way. He calls this "the power of narrative." Through telling stories, he says, a reader can "fit that story into his or her life."

Children, even infants, have the capacity to learn moral behaviour. Adults, too, as they teach their children, continue to hone their moral code. Thus, as parents share stories with their children, everyone's moral intelligence grows. According to Coles, "Stories encourage the moral imagination to work, and they are concrete and connected to everyday experience. Abstract formulations and risks are in one ear and out the next, and even if we memorise them, they don't have the flesh of the daily life. Stories are based on experience." While stories can foster moral intelligence, they won't have much effect if parents and other adults don't set a good example. Any lesson offered a child in an abstract manner that isn't backed up by deeds is not going to work very well. We live out what we presumably want taught to our children. Children are taking constant notice, and they're measuring us not by what we say but what we do.

In what other ways can parents foster moral behaviour in their children? Here are ideas that may help.

- *Be a model of the moral behaviour you want to encourage.* Children learn first and foremost from the example set for them by adults significant in their life. Adolescents and teenagers, especially, are likely to dismiss our pleadings for moral behaviour unless our "walk" is consistent with our "talk." We are unlikely to persuade our kids to be honest if they hear us lying to the boss on the phone.
- *Set and enforce standards for moral behaviour.* A standard is a measure by which we judge our actions. Standards can help young people make decisions about moral behaviour long before a difficult situation presents itself. They often address issues like personal responsibility, sexual behaviour, drug and alcohol use, honesty, integrity, work, respect for others, and fairness. The standards you set may be based on tradition, culture, religious beliefs or some combination.
- *Use reasoning, not force, to encourage compliance.* It's wise to encourage children's voluntary compliance with moral standards and avoid a contest of wills. Parents can achieve this goal by giving reasons and explanations for expected behaviour, appealing to a child's pride and desire to be grown up, and explaining the consequences of behaviour for themselves and others.
- *When violations occur, use victim-oriented discipline strategies.* Just about all young people are bound to violate moral principles on occasion, even if their

parents have diligently taught them right from wrong. Part of helping young people internalise moral behaviour is allowing them to experience the consequences of their actions, especially for others, and requiring them to make amends to the injured party of their wrongdoing.

Guiding Your Children

Wise parents guide their children by creating a "safety net" of appropriate limits. They also encourage desirable behaviour with positive reinforcement, are clear and firm about rules and expectations, explain the reasons behind rules, and enforce the consequences of breaking them. This gentle-but-firm guidance is crucial because it helps children develop an internal sense of self-responsibility and morality.

Setting reasonable limits on children's behaviour provides stability and security. When consequences are consistent, children learn the results of poor choices. Experiencing consequences allows children to "rehearse" better behaviour and understand how to deal with future situations. Parents also should consider each child's personality and maturity when setting reasonable limits and guiding a child to appropriate learning experiences.

Good parents are rarely viewed by their children as dictatorial. In fact, children are more likely to follow parental guidance when it's given in a context of mutual give and take. They're also more likely to be respectful of parents and others when parents share their power, such as taking their children's input seriously in family decisions. Children of parents who wield total authority are actually less likely to comply.

Parental guidance is so vital because it starts children on the path to developing their own sense of morality and responsibility. As you guide and direct your children, remember that children learn by doing, not by having parents do for them. Guiding conveys walking along beside them, showing them the way.

Here are some ideas for guiding children:

- *Explain family rules in advance.* Make sure your children know what's expected of them in advance and the consequences if they break the rules.
- Make sure your children understand that the consequence for name-calling will be a time-out and writing an apology note.
- *Involve your children in setting family rules.* As much as you can, discuss family rules with your children and arrive at an agreement together. Children are more likely to comply with rules they've helped set.
- *Encourage good behaviour with rewards.* Rewarding good behaviour with extra privileges and surprises motivates children better than punishment. For example, if your child has worked hard on chores all morning, you could tell her: "You're such a good worker! Why don't we go out for ice cream when you're done?"
- *Speak in positives.* Young children tend to respond better when they're redirected to a positive behaviour rather than punished for a negative one. For example, instead of saying, "Get away from that vase," say, "Please come over here by me." Instead of saying, "Don't you dare make another mess," say, "Next time remember to pick up your toys, please."
- *Talk it out.* When your children make mistakes, sit down and talk with them. Discuss what they did and what the consequences were. Listen to them. Rehearse with them what they might do differently next time.

- *Teach by example.* Your own behaviour is your children's most influential guide. If you want to teach your children honest, decent, moral behaviour, you must behave honestly, decently, and morally yourself. Consider your personal strengths and weaknesses. What can you improve to become a better example for your children? Set a personal goal to improve in one area that will make you a better role model.
- *Hold family meetings.* Recommended by religious leaders and family experts alike, family meetings provide an opportunity for parents to guide their children. Family meetings can be used to clarify family responsibilities and expectations, set goals, assign chores, resolve problems, and celebrate one another's successes. Good meetings allow each person to voice their opinions, express their feelings, and help in solving problems and making decisions.

Schedule a regular time for family meetings, say the first Sunday of every month. Meetings shouldn't always be used to air concerns and solve problems. Try to talk about fun things, too, like planning a family vacation. Set an agenda and follow it. Before the meeting, encourage family members to add anything to the agenda that they want discussed. You might post a piece of paper on the refrigerator or a bulletin board for this purpose. Rotate conducting the meeting between parents and older children.

Parenting Children with Behaviour Problems

Some children present special parenting challenges. We often label them "difficult" or "disobedient" or even "bad." These children don't intend to try their parents but rather are born with a challenging temperament.

Unfortunately, most young children with behaviour problems provoke negative reactions from adults. These reactions tend to make the child's behaviour worse, starting a harmful pattern that can continue throughout a child's life.

Temperament, Parenting and Behaviour

A child's temperament, or behaviour tendencies, is an inborn trait. Temperament problems can create a negative cycle between parent and child. A child with a difficult temperament behaves badly, and in turn his parents react with ineffective or inconsistent discipline. This cycle has to be broken. Below are parenting habits that can contribute either positively or negatively to this cycle.

- *Modelling*. "Modelling" is learning by watching others. Children tend to do what they see others do. If parents or siblings model bad behaviour, a child is likely to behave badly in the same ways.
- *Reinforcement*. "Reinforcement" is rewarding a child for his behaviour. Sometimes unacceptable behaviour is unintentionally reinforced. For example, parents sometimes laugh at a bad word their child said because it seemed cute or funny. But laughter tends to reinforce a behaviour.
- *Punishment*. It's easy to punish a child out of anger, but this reaction does more harm than good. Harsh punishment or using punishment too often can create feelings of resentment in a child. It also teaches him to obey just to avoid punishment rather than to obey because he understands right from wrong.
- *Reciprocal escalation*. This occurs when parents become aggressive toward their child because the child behaved aggressively. Reciprocal escalation tends to make a bad situation worse.

- *Complementary escalation*. This occurs when parents give in to the demands of a child. Rather than respond appropriately to aggressive behaviour, parents ignore it so they can avoid conflict. Usually the more parents cave in to a child's demands, the more demands the child will come up with.

Strategies for Overcoming Difficult Behaviour

Child development experts suggest a five-step method parents can use to help a child improve difficult behaviour. The steps build on one another, so each one is important.

1. *Attending*. Attending is simply reinforcing desired behaviour by describing it aloud with enthusiasm, such as "Look how high you're stacking your blocks!" or "You're talking with your inside voice." Attending can be a powerful foundation for changing behaviour because it helps parents relate to their child through constant, positive attention. It also improves the parent-child relationship.
2. *Rewarding*. Rewarding is showing a child approval for her good behaviour. Rewarding doesn't take the place of attending but rather adds to it. As parents describe their child's appropriate behaviour, at times they should add rewards and praise.
3. *Ignoring*. Ignoring is a very effective way to reduce a child's unacceptable behaviour, and it is much easier to use than punishment. But ignoring should never be used alone. Instead, once your child stops the unacceptable behaviour, immediately reward him for his now-acceptable behaviour. Ignoring also should not be used when a child's behaviour is potentially dangerous to himself, others, or property. Instead, use more active measures, such as a time-out. Examples of behaviours that can be

ignored include whining, nagging, temper tantrums, and interrupting.

4. *Giving directions*. Parents sometimes give directions that are hard for a young child to follow. "Chain direction," for example, is when a parent gives several directions at once. Instead, parents should give one direction at a time. "Vague directions" aren't specific enough, such as "Behave yourself" or "Be nice." Instead, parents should say exactly what they want their child to do.

5. *Using time-outs*. It takes time to help a child change difficult behaviour. Even if you're using all the right techniques in all the right ways, your child might continue to behave badly, especially at the beginning stages of using a new approach. Time-outs are a helpful consequence for non-compliance, especially when they're used consistently.

Promoting Changes in a Positive Environment

While helping a child change is not easy, it can become easier and more effective when he or she has a positive environment. Parents can do many things to make the environment of their home more positive. You should:

- Have fun with your child.
- Communicate "I love you" often.
- Have structure and routines.
- Participate in family traditions and rituals.
- Be a good listener.
- Request feedback from your child and take turns talking.
- Work on developing patience.

— Build your child's self-esteem.

— Help your child solve problems with peers.

While helping your strong-willed child change his behaviour is not easy, it is very important. The progress may come slowly. It will require much time and patience, and at times you might feel like his behaviour is not improving. When you feel discouraged, it might be easy to slip back into old discipline habits, but it's important to stay constant in your efforts. If you do, you will eventually help your child improve his behaviour and you will strengthen your relationship with him.

Parenting Children with Disabilities

Research about parenting children with disabilities has often focused on the negative aspects, such as family disruption and stress. But many researchers are now saying they've overstated the negatives and overlooked the positives. While families with disabled children do experience challenges, newer studies show that with good support they're as vibrant and healthy as families without disabled children. Many parents, in fact, feel their families have been blessed because of their special child. They say they're closer and have become more compassionate, tolerant, sympathetic, flexible, and selfless.

Strategies for Adjustment and Coping

While each family experiences struggles unique to their child's disability and family situation, the families who report a positive parenting experience tend to share several characteristics in common. Researchers recommend the following based on their findings:

— *Allow a period of grieving.* Every parent expects to have a perfect, healthy child. Disappointment can be acute when you learn your child has a physical or mental disability. You may experience feelings of denial, anxiety, guilt, depression, or even anger. Don't be ashamed of these normal reactions. A period of grieving is natural as you begin the coping process.

— *Maintain a strong marital relationship.* For most couples, their spouse is their greatest source of strength and support. Learning your child has special needs can be traumatic for both of you. Discuss concerns and feelings. Be sensitive to the different ways you might react to the situation.

— *Stay positive and have realistic expectations.* Researchers say that families coping well with a special needs child keep a positive attitude, have realistic expectations of their child, and are less preoccupied with negative thoughts. Understanding the following principles can help you adopt these coping skills.

Your child can't help it. Remind yourself that the problems your child is experiencing come from a special need he or she can't control, not from a personality trait. Anxiety makes things worse. Recognise over-anxiety and calm yourself. It's natural to be concerned about the future of your child, but excessive anxiety can get in the way of making good decisions.

Your child will grow up at his/her own rate. Don't compare your child with another or pressure her to keep up with her peers. She child will grow and learn at her own rate. Keep goals realistic. If expectations are too high, you and your child will be disappointment and may lose motivation.

Helping Your Child

Your child needs your help to maintain self-confidence.

Accept your child as he is. Allow him to feel unconditionally loved because of who he is—not what he achieves. Finding the root cause won't change the situation. Parents often want desperately to know what caused their child's disability. While this information can be helpful, the present and future are more important. If your priority is to accept your child and her needs rather than understand what went wrong, you'll be better able to provide educational and emotional support. Negative thinking makes the situation worse. It takes energy to stay in negative thinking about a difficult situation. Use your energy for positive action.

Celebrate your child's strengths as they emerge. Take pride in your child's strengths and positive characteristics. Emphasise what she can do rather than what she can't. Encouraging her helps her recognise her abilities and develop healthy self-esteem.

Turn to religious faith for strength. Religious faith and beliefs provide many families with strength, support, and hope during times of difficulty. Belief in a divine plan allows many fathers and mothers to find meaning in their situation and to rise above discouragement. Many parents see their special needs child as a divine son or daughter of God and believe it's a blessing to be entrusted with this special spirit in their home. They feel their child was sent to them for a purpose. You can draw hope and strength from knowing that you have "a sacred duty to rear [your] children in love and righteousness, to provide for their physical and spiritual needs, to teach them to love and serve one another, to observe the commandments of God and to be law-abiding citizens wherever they live".

Actively seek support. You don't have to face a challenging parenting situation alone. Join a parent support group where you can share experiences and worries with others in a similar situation. Educate relatives, friends, or neighbours about your child's disability and communicate your needs and feelings. Most will be anxious to help and only need you to tell them how. Also, you don't have to reinvent the wheel. Many programmes and services can help. Actively seeking support can greatly decrease stress and anxiety for you and your family. Begin by talking with doctors, schools counsellors, and religious leaders. You may even have a neighbour or close friend who can recommend a particular service, web site, or professional.

Increase understanding and love among siblings. Having a sibling with a disability can present unique challenges for children. Attention and energy can sometimes become too focused on the special needs child. Be sensitive to the needs of your children who are siblings to a special needs child. Allow them to talk freely about their feelings. Do your best to help them understand their sibling's disability. Teach them how to help when they see their sibling in need. Discuss together ways to handle difficult situations.

Enhance resiliency. Children learn by example. You can help them become more resilient by being a role model of resilient behaviour. As you react in healthy ways, problem-solve, persevere, and adapt to stressful situations, your children will learn these same skills. They'll notice your strength as you advocate on their behalf to schools and doctors. Along with setting an example, give your children opportunities to practice resiliency skills, such as making choices and experiencing consequences.

Be an advocate. Studies show that parents who report coping well with their special needs child also report advocating for their child. Advocating means speaking up with teachers, doctors, and specialists to make sure your special needs child gets good care. Learn all you can about your child's disability. Research the programmes and services available to you. Evaluate what doctors, specialists, or teachers tell you. If they're not providing quality services, know your options and seek alternatives.

7

Parenting of Adolescents

When babies arrive in the world, they are tiny, helpless people who depend entirely on adults to take care of all their needs and wants. Somehow, with the proper loving nurturing and care over the next 22 years, they grow to become independent adults who can take care of themselves and others. The journey from infancy to adulthood is an amazing time when children soak up everything in the world around them and mix it with the qualities they are born with in order to mature bit by bit, in every way.

Children must pass through several stages, or take specific steps, on their road to becoming adults. For most people, there are four or five such stages of growth where they learn certain things: infancy (birth to age two), early childhood (ages 3 to 8 years), later childhood (ages 9 to 12) and adolescence (ages 13 to 18). Persons 18 and over are considered adults in our society. Of course, there are some who will try to act older than their years. But, for the most part, most everybody grows in this same pattern. Parents learn much about taking care of their babies and young children. At the hospital or with the doctor, you might pick up information about what to feed them or how long they should sleep. Later, school staff may remind you about the importance of talking and reading to your young children. You can also see how your friends or relatives treat their kids. You cannot say the same thing about learning to talk with teenagers (adolescents). It seems like everyone, even teachers and neighbours, have problems understanding them. Giving up, you might turn to doing and saying the same things your parents did with you. But those were other times!

You can begin to understand this age group if you look at its place on the growth sequence. Notice how it's right next to the adult stage, the last step before being an adult. This is a time for adolescents to decide about their future line of work and think about starting their own families in a few years. One of the first things they must do is to start making their own decisions. For example, adolescents can begin to decide what to buy with their own money or who will be their friend. To do this, they must put a little distance between themselves and their parents. This does not mean that you can't continue to "look after them" or help them when needed. You should, as much as possible, let them learn from the results of their actions. Adolescents also need to be around other adults, both male and female. These can be relatives, neighbours, or teachers. Of course, they should be positive role models. Your teenagers can learn from them about things like how to fix the car, getting along with others, or ideas for future jobs. Finally, don't worry if they want to spend time alone. Adolescents can "spend hours" day dreaming about their future life. They might be planning the things they can do or will buy "when they grow up." Remember, to travel far, one begins with the first few steps!

Parenting teens is a monumental task, with a few parenting bumps in the road and many rewards. Parenting a teenager is not easy—it takes creativity, determination, and patience! It's a tough journey, but you don't have to take it alone. Although there is no magic spell that will make teens act differently, you can achieve the same drastic change by learning how to deal with and approach your teenager in order to get the results you want.

Although teenagers will make their own choices, a good home life can increase the odds that kids will avoid many of the pitfalls of adolescence. Particularly, a kind, warm, solid relationship with parents who demonstrate respect for their children, an interest in their children's activities, and set firm boundaries for those activities may directly or indirectly deter criminal activity, illegal drug and alcohol use, negative peer pressure, delinquency, sexual promiscuity, and low self-esteem.

Parents who give their teenagers their love, time, boundaries, and encouragement to think for themselves may find that they actually enjoy their children's adventure through adolescence. As they watch their sons and daughters grow in independence, make decisions, and develop into young adults, they may find that the child they have reared is—like the breathtaking view of the newborn they held for the first time—even better than they could have imagined.

Monitoring the Teens

Raising teens in today's world can be a daunting challenge. They're vulnerable to dangers that lurk around many corners, whether the corner is at home or miles away. Dangers to younger children are mostly centred near home. As children get older, the dangers multiply and become harder to anticipate. Parents often feel helpless because they can't keep up the same level of vigilance as they could when their children were smaller. Teen children cannot be in sight at all moments.

With teens, a different kind of vigilance is needed. Call it "monitoring" or "keeping tabs," but don't think it requires any less effort. Parents can—and must—watch over their teens with continuing vigilance. The older the child, the more your monitoring will become oversight rather than direct sight, but it is just as important.

Monitoring means supervising your teens. It means knowing your teens' whereabouts at all times, who they spend time, and all their social plans. It also includes being aware of your teenager's behaviour when he or she is not in your sight, such as during school hours.

Despite the increasing challenges, monitoring is one of the most important things a parent can do to prevent adolescent problem behaviour. Research shows that better parental monitoring is related to lower rates of sexual activity, drug and alcohol use, truancy, thoughts about suicide and suicide attempts, running away and delinquency. One study showed that only 8 percent of ninth graders whose parents monitored their activities closely were likely to have had five alcoholic drinks in a row during the past month, compared with 68 percent of ninth graders whose parents didn't keep close tabs on them. A similar trend was noted for sexual activity.

To be an effective monitor, you don't need to be present at every moment. You also don't have to become overly intrusive or violate the privacy that teens typically crave. You do need to show consistent and active interest in your child's life. And you do need to be willing to enforce family rules and raise issues that concern you.

In one family a dispute came up when the 14-year-old daughter told her parents she wanted to go to a high school dance. Her parents thought she was too young, and they proposed that instead she give a party at their house. She thought that was a dumb idea, but she couldn't come up with an alternative that both she and her parents felt good about. Since they couldn't agree, family rules dictated that she go by her parents' wishes. She gave the party. To her surprise, she and her friends had a great time.

Rules and Boundaries

Family rules and boundaries can provide a sense of stability to teens who are struggling to decipher relationships, roles, and even their own personalities. Although they may protest loudly against being required to live up to certain standards, when they have a hand in crafting those standards, and when those standards are demanding but fair, teenagers will flourish. Having something steady, firm, and predictable in a head spinning world is like being handed a map, with north plainly marked. Clear boundaries and standards are the gauge by which all other information is measured.

Disciplining teenagers is difficult, but it is critical if teens are to learn that their behaviour has consequences. Some of the odiousness of enforcing rules can be eliminated by engaging children in the process of setting the rules and assigning consequences *before* the rules are broken. When parents include teenagers in establishing clear rules about appropriate behaviour and consequences, the arguments over rules and punishment end. Children can no longer claim that punishments or expectations are unfair, and parents can take on the role of calmly enforcing the pre-arranged consequences instead of having to impress upon the child the seriousness of the problem and scramble to find an appropriate punishment.

The temptation to react emotionally when children break rules is alleviated because a breach of the rules is no longer perceived as an assault on parental authority, since it is by the authority of the family, not the authority of the parents, that the rules were established. Helping to set the rules may not dissuade teenagers from breaking them sometimes, but it can help parents to avoid a power struggle with their teenagers.

Another big trap in parent-teen relationships is the confusion of psychological control (the opposite of psychological autonomy) with discipline. Demanding a certain level of behaviour of children does not exclude allowing, or even encouraging them to think and express opinions different than one's own. Too many parents get caught up in focusing on controlling their child, believing that controlling the way their child thinks will translate into controlling what their child does. By using guilt, withdrawing love, or invalidating feelings or beliefs, the parent hopes to make the child see things the parent's way, ensuring compliance with parental expectations.

There is a fine line here; one of the roles of parents is to help children make sense of the world by offering explanations or interpretations of events. It is when these parental offerings take on the tone of exclusiveness—when parents cannot respectfully consider and discuss a teenager's interpretation of his or her own experience—that psychological control has taken over.

Parents should also be aware that it is the teenager's perspective on the forcefulness of the suggestion which counts. Psychological control is damaging if it is perceived by the teenager, regardless of parental intention. While a parent may feel that a discussion has taken on the tone of a healthy debate, to a teenager the same interchange can feel absolutely crushing. Interestingly, boys are more likely to report that their parents squelch their psychological autonomy than are girls. Whether this is a difference in the way parents actually relate to teenage boys versus teenage girls, or whether it is a difference in perception of boys versus girls is unclear.

When discipline becomes a matter of calmly enforcing family rules about behaviour, many of the problems associated with psychological control are alleviated. When children have a problem with delinquency, parents generally tend to respond to it with less behavioural control, and more psychological control as time goes by. This appears to set-up a vicious cycle, as teenagers respond to both lack of monitoring and the presence of psychological control by acting out, or becoming more delinquent.

If parents can break this cycle by treating delinquent behaviour with increased monitoring rather than attempting to control it by inducing guilt, withdrawing love, or other means of psychological control, teenagers are more likely to respond with better behaviour. In short, parents who concentrate on trying to control their child's behaviour rather than trying to control their child are going to have much more success and a lot less grief.

Developing Close Relationships with Teens

Parents would do well to concentrate on a three-pronged approach to managing the journey.

First, a positive relationship with their child is essential to success. When parent-child interactions are characterised by warmth, kindness, consistency, respect, and love, the relationship will flourish, as will self-esteem, mental health, spirituality, and social skills.

Second, being genuinely interested in children's activities allows parents to monitor behaviour, which is crucial in keeping teens out of trouble. When misbehaviour does occur, parents who have involved their children in setting family rules and consequences can expect less flack from their children as they calmly enforce the rules. Parents who, together with their children, set firm boundaries and high expectations may find that their children's abilities to live up to those expectations grow.

Third, parents who encourage independent thought and expression in their children may find that they are raising children who have a healthy sense of self and an enhanced ability to resist peer pressure.

Parents who give their teenagers their love, time, boundaries, and encouragement to think for themselves may find that they actually enjoy their children's adventure through adolescence. As they watch their sons and daughters grow in independence, make decisions, and develop into young adults, they may find that the child they have reared is, like the breathtaking view of the newborn they held for the first time, even better than they could have imagined.

In an era of increased drug use, teenage pregnancy and youth suicide, it's little wonder that most parents are very concerned about their teens. Very often they ask: "How can I protect my teens from these things?" An important key is to develop close, caring relationships with teenagers.

Teenagers who have close relationships with their parents are less likely to use drugs, abuse alcohol or become pregnant out of wedlock. These teens are more likely to adopt the beliefs and values of their parents. Teens who are close to their parents resist peer pressure better and are less likely to commit crimes.

How do we develop close relationships with our teens? Here are some ideas from experts in adolescent development.

- *Be honest.* Adolescents are developing their thinking abilities. They want to know the reasons for everything, and they expect consistency from their parents. They are critical of the parent who is dishonest or two-faced.
- *Be open.* Adolescents want to be able to talk with their parents, but they also need their privacy and independence. The adult-adolescent conversation

needs to be two-sided, with both people sharing their thoughts and feelings. Adolescents want to know if, as adults, we are struggling over the same concerns they are. If we are doing most of the talking, we're talking too much.

— When it is your turn to speak, watch your language. Sometimes we talk to teens in ways that say "you would be OK if..." or "we will love you more if..."(... you go to church, clean your room, get good grades, etc.).

— We order, warn, nag, threaten and preach to our teens to try to teach them to be more responsible and more sensible. However, this can backfire and actually encourage our teens to be less responsible and less sensible. Teens are more likely to be responsible and follow our wishes if they feel accepted. Speaking politely conveys acceptance. For example, we can say, "I'm sorry to interrupt you, but..." or "I realise you may not want to, but it would help me so much if..."

— Also, catching teens doing the things we want and praising them for it fosters feelings of acceptance. For example, instead of praising them for "a nice report card", say "You've done very well in art and science. You must really like those subjects."

— *Be calm.* Adolescents like to try out their arguing skills. If you get angry and yell or scream, this is an ideal time for them to practice. Avoid getting into power struggles and arguments with your adolescent. If you talk calmly, your child can see you as in control of the situation.

— *Set clear and consistent limits.* Younger children abide by the rules set down by the parents just because they are rules. Adolescents are more likely to question the importance of the rule and why there has to be one at all. You should respect your child's need to have the rule explained. Take time to explain why this rule is set and allow time for negotiation of certain rules such as curfew. However, don't hesitate to say when something is not open to negotiation, such as riding in a car with kids who have been drinking or taking drugs.

— Remember that growing up means becoming independent. In situations where your child's well-being is not in danger, you may need to accept that your child makes choices you wouldn't have made. Or that your child has behaved in ways that you don't approve. That's independence. Your child may temporarily dress weird or follow a strange hairstyle trend. Your teen is showing individualism and independence from you. Try to overlook some of the outside appearances and concentrate on the inner strengths of your teenager. When teens plan a party, leave the planning to them and don't interfere unless asked or unless the plans become unacceptable to you.

— *Be supportive.* Independence does not mean isolation. It means establishing a different kind of relationship with parents, not terminating it. Almost all adolescents say their parents are the most important people in their lives. Adolescence is a time when you are needed—when teens are trying to figure out who they really are.

No matter how frustrated you may feel at times, your teen needs you as a base of support, as much now as during the early years of life.

Disciplining with Love

According to parenting scholars, parents use three major

approaches to win their children's compliance: coercion, love withdrawal, and induction. Parents who use coercion attempt to force their will on their child through hostile or severely punitive means, such as yelling, ordering, hitting, or demeaning. While such strategies often yield compliance, research shows that parents who frequently use them produce children who lack social ability, are withdrawn, lack spontaneity, are more aggressive, and have an underdeveloped conscience.

Parents who use love withdrawal show disapproval and suspend their loving attention until the behaviour changes. For example, they might refuse to talk to their child until she complies. Research on the effectiveness of this approach shows mixed results, but they do indicate a child may suffer from excessive guilt if frequently disciplined this way.

Induction includes reasoning with children and explaining the effects of their behaviour on others. It uses patience and gentle persuasion to encourage desired behaviour. Experts say induction is a far healthier form of discipline than either coercion or love withdrawal. Parents who regularly use induction produce children who have better-developed consciences and are more socially competent, responsible, internally motivated to make good choices, independent, confident, and achievement-oriented.

Sometimes, however, simple reasoning is not enough to win compliance. On these occasions, parents may be tempted to yell, threaten, or ground their child. Invoking consequences is a better alternative. When parents allow children to experience the direct results of their choices, rather than shielding them from these results, children learn for themselves that certain actions produce certain outcomes. The emphasis is on teaching the child, not punishing him.

It's important for parents to set-up in advance the consequences that will logically follow from a particular misbehaviour. For example, a teen who breaks curfew loses the use of the family car for a predetermined amount of time. A child who goes to visit friends without telling his parents first loses the privilege of spending time with friends for a time. When there isn't a clear connection between a misbehaviour and a consequence, parents are likely punishing rather than teaching.

In order for consequences to be effective, they must be given in the spirit of guiding and teaching. Discipline should be delivered in the context of a love and tender concern for a child's long-term welfare. Parents should have a sincere interest in teaching children correct principles and not see disciplining as an opportunity to vent or take revenge. Parental authority should never be mistaken for the opportunity to command or abuse.

Some parents insist on harsh punishment or immediately assign consequences for misbehaviour. But it is important to understand the reasons behind a child's misbehaviour before deciding on discipline. Sometimes a child behaves badly because of a disorder that requires medical attention. Perhaps a child is acting out to gain attention, meet an unfilled need, or express fear or worry. A teen might be late getting home from an evening outing because he helped a stranded motorist. Reacting with immediate punishment or assignment of consequences in these situations would probably be counterproductive. Parents should sincerely try to understand their children's behaviour rather than simply react to it. With understanding, parents can provide more effective discipline and be better teachers to their children. Full understanding of the circumstances surrounding bad behaviour can also help parents plan ahead to prevent potential problems. After being corrected, children often have a particularly strong need to feel their parents' love. Children need to know that they are still loved and valued, even when they misbehave. Wise parents follow up discipline by assuring children they are loved and cared for.

In short, the best discipline style avoids harshness and minimises reprimands. It is a careful balance between reasonable strictness and unconditional love and acceptance. Effective discipline is always delivered within the context of a loving parent-child relationship.

Here are practical suggestions for disciplining with love:

— *Calm down*. Correct children when you're calm and collected, not when you're frustrated and angry. If you catch yourself about to discipline with anger, take a deep breath, stop, and count to 30. Or send your child to his room and go to your own bedroom to compose yourself and think about the situation.

— *Strive to understand your child's misbehaviour before you discipline*. Is your daughter acting out because she is tired, restless, or anxious for attention? Maybe a nap or some extra time with you would be more beneficial than punishment. Is your son in a freedom-seeking stage of growth (typically the two's, three's, and the teenage years)? What can you do to help him seek independence safely and responsibly? Is something in the environment bothering him? Perhaps he's lost a favourite toy or he's afraid of the dark or he performed poorly on an exam. Maybe your child just didn't know better. If so, teach him rather than punish him.

— *Use consequences*. Consequences teach children how their actions affect their own and others' lives. Consequences work better than threats and nagging. They're especially effective if your children are included in deciding what consequences should follow what misbehaviour. For example:

Before children go out, many parents have a routine of asking the Who-What-Where-When questions: Who are you going to be with? What you will be doing? Where you will be? What time will you be home? They agree together on the answers. Any changes in plans must be approved by a phone call. Otherwise friend privileges are lost for a time.

Most parents assign their children chores, often with the expectation they'll be done before dinner. If they complain about doing their chores, they can be asked to go to their rooms until they agree to comply. Otherwise they miss dinner.

- *Look for alternatives to spanking and physical punishment.* Options include withdrawing privileges (unsafe driving will result in not being allowed to use the car for one week), emphasising the damage or pain caused ("You made your sister so sad when you called her that," or "This has really damaged my trust in you."), and requiring restitution (apologising, working to repair damaged property or injured relationships).
- *Continue to love.* When discipline is given, make sure you follow it with love and affection. Assure your children that even when you don't like what they do, you still love them. Express confidence in them.

Nurture Healthy Food Habits

Your child's nutrition is important to her overall health. Proper nutrition can also prevent many medical problems, including becoming overweight, developing weak bones, and developing diabetes. It will also ensure that your child physically grows to her full potential.

The best nutrition advise to keep your adolescent healthy includes encouraging her to:

- Eat a variety of foods
- Balance the food you eat with physical activity
- Choose a diet with plenty of grain products, vegetables and fruits
- Choose a diet low in fat, saturated fat, and cholesterol
- Choose a diet moderate in sugars and salt
- Choose a diet that provides enough calcium and iron to meet their growing body's requirements.

You can also help promote good nutrition by setting a good example. Healthy eating habits and regular exercise should be a regular part of your family's life. It is much easier if everyone in the house follows these guidelines, than if your child has to do it alone. You should also buy low-calorie and lowfat meals, snacks and desserts, low fat or skim milk and diet drinks. Avoid buying high calorie desserts or snacks, such as snack chips, regular soft drinks or regular ice cream.

Ensure proper nutrition (eating three meals a day and two nutritious snacks, limiting high sugar and high fat foods, eating fruits, vegetables, lean meats and low fat dairy products, including 3 servings of milk, cheese or yogurt to meet their calcium needs), regular exercise, adequate sleep (10-11 hours each night), and participation in extracurricular activities at school and in the community.

- Limit television viewing and encourage reading.

- Practice food safety: washing fruits and vegetables and not eating under-cooked meats or poultry.
- Brush teeth with a fluoride toothpaste twice a day and have your child seen regularly by a dentist. Encourage flossing each day.
- Supervise your child's use of the computer (a child at this age should not have unsupervised access to the Internet), computer games, movies, and know what they have access to at their friends' homes.
- Prepare your child for puberty and sexual development and begin sexuality education if you have not already done so, including that abstinence is the safest way to prevent pregnancy and sexually transmitted diseases.

It is also very important to begin communicating with your child to help prevent them from picking up bad habits, including the use of tobacco, alcohol and drugs (including the use of inhalants; especially aerosols and glue). Children whose parents talk to them regularly are at much less risk for experimenting with cigarettes, alcohol and drugs. Teach them how to avoid situations where drugs, alcohol, or cigarettes are present and to choose friends who also choose not to use these substances. Emphasise to them that these substances can hurt them, can make them sick, can cause decrease lung function and problems playing sports, and that it is OK to say no. Also, do not let them attend parties that are unsupervised by adults and let your child know that they can communicate openly with you about these difficult subjects. Watch for the warning signs of drug use, including a sudden change in your child's behaviour or personality, decreased performance in school, or changes in what friends they associate with.

In addition to teaching your children to avoid cigarettes, a new hazard is the increasing use of cigarettes, which are imported from India, are unfiltered and come in various flavours. Although marketed as a safe alternative to regular cigarettes, bidis are even more hazardous, and although they contain less tobacco, they produce more nicotine, tar and carbon dioxide than regular cigarettes, and should be avoided by your children. You should also educate your children that bidi, cigarettes are not herbal or tobacco free as many adolescents believe.

How to Deal with Stubborn Teenagers?

The teenage years is a very difficult period not only for you as the parent but for you teenager as well. Most parents would ask how to deal with stubborn teenagers since this age is really where independence and individuality is cultivated. But you need not worry about this stage, a lot of parents have gone through their child's own teenage years and most of them have actually succeeded.

Here are some hints on how to deal with stubborn teenagers:

- One way to deal with stubborn teenagers is to listen very carefully—most parents are not aware of it, but stubborn teenagers can actually result from stubborn parents. After puberty, most kids think they are already adults ready to face the world; luckily, parents are wise enough to know that this is not true. However, parents may think too little of their teens to a point that they still treat them as kids whose ideas are just kid stuff.
- The truth of the matter is, the teenager is more mature than kids, albeit still not mature enough—this means that your teenager may have something to say about themselves or the way they wish to be

treated. Listen to what they say first before saying what you think. Oftentimes, parents just stubbornly and automatically deflect anything their teens have to say, this in turn makes the teenager just act like their stubborn parents and become stubborn teenagers.

- When stubborn teenagers give their perspective, acknowledge it even if you do not agree. It is important for stubborn teenagers to know that you have heard their opinion on things. But you do not necessarily have to follow it or agree with it, after all, in most cases, your teen may just be asking for your advice or if you have other ideas in mind. After acknowledging your teen's idea it is then you can say what you think should be.
- To deal with stubborn teenagers, imagine yourself in your teenager's shoes. You were also a teenager years or decades ago and you should know how difficult such times were. But do not dwell too much on your own experiences because your teen is probably facing different challenges in life. A lot of parents say things like "I know better because I have been there" in hopes of preventing their children from doing something. But that is actually an invitation for the child to be even more curious of such circumstances.
- Another way to deal with stubborn teenagers is to avoid making use of labels when talking to your child, especially during arguments. Labels might sound meaningless when you blurt them out, but they can easily get into your teenager's mind whether the label is positive or negative. It is important to allow your teenager to let him or her self be without labels being attached. Otherwise, stubbornness might stem from your teenager's effort to veer away from the labels.

— Try to avoid debating with your child about matters of opinion. Even if debates occur to convince a party of your opinion, what it actually does is to strengthen the other party's hold on their opinion as both of you create reasons for believing your stand. In this case it is better to show why your opinion might be better and allow your teenager to see for himself or herself what makes you think you are right.

Stubbornness is somewhat inevitable for teenagers, but it might actually be a necessary trait at this point where they are developing their identities. What matters is that you are there for them at this critical stage with much love and understanding. With an open mind and a sound heart you would be able to know how to deal with stubborn teenagers.

How to Raise Drug-free Teens?

While there are many tough issues when raising teens that can strike fear in the heart of a parent, teen drug use might be number one. But parents can't allow fears to force them to ignore drug concerns in their teen's life—and all teens have them! Each and every teenager knows someone in school who experiments or readily uses drugs. Every teen has seen it on television or in the news.

To empower a drug-free teen you'll need to put your fear aside and meet this issue head on. You can keep your teen drug-free, or start them on a drug-free path if they have been experimenting already, because this issue is not bigger than your loving influence.

While your teen is learning to become independent, you will still need to guide the way. This is especially true when it comes to serious issues like drug use because it is not just your teen you are dealing with. There are the drug dealers who would love to get to your child or the negative peers who would use your child to valid their drug using behaviour. Therefore, it is very important you make a conscience effort to set the rules where teen drug use is concerned.

Tell your teen that drug use of any kind will not be tolerated in your family. Be clear so that there is no interpretation. Ask if he understands these expectations.

Ask your teen if there are any questions. Be prepared to answer these and bring up a few of your own if you feel more information needs to be discussed. Continue talking to your teen about drugs after the rules have been set.

Establish the consequences for breaking the rules. Be firm with them. Once these are set, think of the consequences as black and white—no gray area here. Don't let your teen off the hook or add consequences when a rule is broken.

Check up on your teenager. When he tells you his plans, check them with other parents. Let your teen know that you take the role as his parent very seriously

Tips to Prevent Your Teen from Taking Drugs

When it comes to teen drug use, an ounce of prevention is worth so much more than a pound of cure. Follow these tips on preventing teen drug use and you will enjoy a drug-free family.

1. *Be there for your teen when he needs to get out of a bad situation.* Be the scapegoat: 'I can't do that, my parents would kill me!' Or be the parent who will pick up your teen without repercussions if he finds the party he's gone too has drugs available or her date has been drinking.
2. *Get to know your teen's friends and their parents on a first name basis.* This will help you know what your

teen is doing and you may make a good friend to boot!

3. *Keep connected in the after school hours.* If you can't be home with your teen, call and leave notes. Have another adult supervise your teen or sign him up for an after school programme. If these things aren't possible, establish a routine for your teenager and keep him busy during this time.
4. *Talk to your teen often about drugs.* Use ice breakers from television shows or the radio in the car. Remember these are conversations, not lectures.
5. *Get your teen involved in extracurricular activities. Schools* offer sports or clubs and community organisations offer classes and youth groups. These will help him mold his identity in a positive way and give him less time doing nothing and becoming bored. Studies have shown teens that have less time to just hang out are less likely to do drugs.
6. *Ask questions when your teen makes plans to go out.* Who will he be with, where is he going, what will he be doing, etc. Then check up on him. Call other parents and do this together.
7. *Be a role model.* If you drink, drink responsibly—and don't ever use illegal drugs.
8. *Unite your family against drugs using strong family beliefs.* Establish that your family doesn't use drugs. Not that you will shun your child should he make a mistake, but that your family believes there are other healthier ways to enjoy life and fix problems rather than escaping into a drug haze.
9. *Connect with your teen by doing things together as a family.* Make this a routine outing and have your

teen help plan it. Eat family meals together. Studies have shown that kids who enjoy dinner together with their parents on a normal basis are less likely to become involved with drugs.

10. *Drop any baggage you may be carrying*. Don't allow the mistakes you made as a teenager or young adult to influence your teen in a negative way. Tap into the mature adult you've become and let the past go.

Other Books on

GENERAL SERIES

1.	Art of Joyful Living **(New)**	160/-
2.	Chanakya Neeti **(New)**	175/-
3.	Helpline for Stressed Parents **(New)**	175/-
4.	Grow Rich with Peace of Mind **(New)**	175/-
5.	How to be Fit and Young **(New)**	175/-
6.	How to Succeed in Life **(New)**	175/-
7.	100 Ways to Develop Self Confidence	175/-
8.	Child Development	225/-
9.	Abraham Lincoln A Complete Biography	225/-
10.	Mein Kampf My Struggle	225/-
11.	Think and Grow Rich	160/-
12.	The Art of Personality Development	150/-
13.	Positive Mind Power	160/-
14.	Travel & Tourism An Industry Facilitator	295/-
15.	World's Great Authors And Poets	150/-
16.	Effective Editing Help Yourself in Becoming a Good Editor	150/-
17.	Smart House-Keeping for Modern Women	195/-
18.	Develop Super Power Memory	175/-
19.	World's Great Personalities	195/-
20.	Personality Plus	150/-
21.	Power of Positive Thinking	160/-
22.	Art of Successful Parenting	225/-
23.	A Handbook of Etiquettes	125/-
24.	World's Great Scientists	195/-
25.	Body Language	175/-
26.	Art of Successful Living	175/-
27.	Jokes for All	150/-

28.	Selected Dohas	350/-
29.	Baby Names for Girls **(New)**	150/-
30.	Baby Names for Boys **(New)**	150/-
31.	Art of Public Speaking	160/-
32.	The World's Greatest Speeches	175/-
33.	Group Discussions	125/-
34.	Personality Development	125/-
35.	Think Positive & Things Will Go Right	125/-
36.	Once in a Blue Moon (A Tantra Tale)	125/-
37.	God is Dead	125/-
38.	Travel India (A Complete Guide for Tourists)	350/-
39.	Glimpses of Urdu Poetry	450/-
40.	How to Reduce Tension	125/-
41.	A Book of Stenography	295/-
42.	Baby Names for the Boy	150/-
43.	Baby Names for the Girl	150/-
44.	Ripples in Tranquil Waters	195/-

Lotus PRESS

Unit No. 220, 2nd Floor, 4735/22, Prakash Deep Building,
Ansari Road, Darya Ganj, New Delhi- 110002
Ph.: 23280047, 9811594448
• E-mail : lotuspress1984@gmail.com, www.lotuspress.co.in